Also by Stephen Lancaster

True Casefiles of a Paranormal Investigator

About the Author

Stephen Lancaster (Lonaconing, Maryland) is a paranormal researcher who has been investigating testaments of the supernatural since 1997. He is the producer of *MonsterVisionTV*, an independent paranormal investigation program with nearly two million viewers worldwide. He has conducted investigative work for politicians, military facilities, the board of education, museums, commercial locations, businesses, television, and civilians. Stephen appeared on A&E Biography's *My Ghost Story* in 2011 and again in 2012. He has been interviewed on hundreds of radio shows, including *Coast To Coast*, *Dark Matters Radio*, and *Darkness Radio*. In 2012, he released the book *Paranormal Investigator: True Casefiles of a Paranormal Investigator*. Stephen has also appeared on various news broadcasts revolving around paranormal phenomena and often gives public lectures on the subject. Stephen is currently producing a documentary titled *Visitant: The Johnson Family Haunting*.

Visit him online at monstervisiontv.net, facebook.com/monsterVisionTV, facebook.com/authorstephenlancaster, or twitter.com/wraithwrite.

STEPHEN LANCASTER

A MAN TERRORIZED BY
THE SUPERNATURAL

Llewellyn Worldwide
Woodbury, Minnesota

FIRST EDITION
First Printing, 2016

Book design by Bob Gaul
Cover image by iStockphoto.com/19595534©Alexander Chernyakov
Cover design by Ellen Lawson
Editing by Gabrielle Rose Simons

Llewellyn Publications is a registered trademark of Llewellyn Worldwide Ltd.

Library of Congress Cataloging-in-Publication Data
Names: Lancaster, Stephen, 1977– author.
Title: Dark spirits : a man terrorized by the supernatural / Stephen Lancaster.
Description: First Edition. | Woodbury, Minnesota :
   Llewellyn Publications, 2016.
Identifiers: LCCN 2016007317 (print) | LCCN 2016011121 (ebook) | ISBN
   9780738738956 | ISBN 9780738749044 ()
Subjects: LCSH: Parapsychology—Case studies.
Classification: LCC BF1029 .L35 2016 (print) | LCC BF1029 (ebook) | DDC
   130—dc23
LC record available at http://lccn.loc.gov/2016007317

Llewellyn Publications
A Division of Llewellyn Worldwide Ltd.
2143 Wooddale Drive
Woodbury, MN 55125-2989
www.llewellyn.com

Printed in the United States of America

Contents

Introduction

They say the moment before you die, your entire life flashes before your eyes. What if those memories never stop flashing? What if those memories are the very origin of the afterlife? Surely there has to be an explanation for the thousands upon thousands of supernatural reports that occur each year. Belief in incorporeal beings has been publically acknowledged since the dawn of time.

Not much has changed over the years, as we sit in the twenty-first century experiencing similar phenomena. For years, I studied the possibility that the memories from our lives perform as an infinite loop—inside of a realm we have yet to understand or even come close to discovering—after death.

The human brain documents our lives and stores those significant and paramount memories. What happens to all of that stored information once we die? It is commonly known that energy from the human body never dies. Energy in itself cannot die, but ultimately and indefinitely changes form. These are scientific facts. This is the part that truly intrigues me and may hold the key to finding the source of ghostly phenomenology.

The electricity or energy from our bioelectrical makeup transfers somewhere and into something after we pass on. Could this energy be the cause of what we know as spirits, clairvoyance, psychic phenomena, déjà vu, telekinesis, and possession? I believe this is certainly an infallible circumstance. The ghosts we experience appear in every shape and form. We have seen children, adults, and even monsters.

With that being said, I want you to consider this: the phantom memory theory that I am speaking of, in which we are physically able to witness the memories of the deceased in three-dimensional, audible forms, could promote an alternate formation of the supernatural.

In many cases, we may be observing the same ghost. A spirit we once thought to be a child is now an adult, and so on and so forth. We may very well be experiencing the memories and the life of any given entity, when exposed to a haunting. They might show us a fond memory of their childhood. They might show us another person or loved one, or even something tragic. Memories are limitless, as are the possibilities of the stories they could tell.

That most indubitably removes most of the sensitivity and intimacy often stapled to sightings of ghosts, and most people would not like that. However, if everything we ever knew pertaining to ghosts would change into something without emotion, personality, or conscious—that to me would create an entity far more terrifying.

This would certainly explain why it is so difficult to arrive at a conclusion on any particular case. With all of these fragments and all of this randomness, how can anyone even consider calling anything a fact with a straight face?

Many colleagues in the field might argue that their data proves spirits can and do communicate with the living on an intelligent level. Whether it is phantom voices or curious visual anomalies in recordings that allude to intelligent afterlife, a percentage of researchers conclude that ghosts are aware.

But you have to consider the brain of an average human being. Think about how many memories you will have by the time of your death. Also consider that memories encompass everything you have ever learned. That is an abundance of data stored in the human brain in a lifetime.

So you have to ask yourself, statistically speaking, could everything and anything an entity could possibly say relate to you, simply because of chance? The answer to that question is, "Yes."

I could ask if you know a certain person by their first name. I might not even be speaking of the person you know, but you do in fact know someone by that name. Our friends, our loved ones, our life experiences, and those of others all end up as memories. The stories we read and the movies we see all end as memories. Any relation to the questions we ask is misunderstood or mere coincidence.

Ghosts and monsters are the very fabric that channel human fear. Fear is balanced by the process of education, learning, and cognition. Is it safe to say that the majority of our own personal fears derived from childhood? We are taught when to fear and how to fear by means of what others already believe. But why does the fear of ghosts and monsters linger well into our adulthood?

If we compare this to a more positive belief, such as the youthfully confident knowledge that Santa Claus exists, one has to wonder at what point in our lives we realized the actual truth that he does not. Somebody told us he did and then later somebody told us he did not. At that point it, was up for us to decide whether we believed or we didn't. In my personal opinion, I think the continued fear of ghosts is well rooted in not fully understanding the unknown. By nature, most people fear what they don't or can't understand.

Since the beginning, human beings have tied the supernatural to everyday occurrences. One example that comes to mind is religion. Many belief structures are dripping with paranormal situations. Fear, belief, ghosts, and goblins all begin in our mind. There is a monster under your bed, and that notion started in your head.

The origins of ghosts and intimidating creatures all began with the thought that created them that resulted in a memory that refused to go away. Am I saying we are all certifiable? I am not insinuating that at all. What I am saying is that ghosts are past, present, and future. Are they all cinema-quality horrific? No. There are countless cases of individuals who experienced positive hauntings or blissful encounters with the deceased.

However, to be fair, there are those that are dangerous and will hurt you. Imagine playing the role of a violent memory and consider that sometimes we are in the wrong place at the right time. Dark, or if I dare use the word "evil," entities are often misconstrued and labeled as demonic or some other monstrosity. I refuse to set labels simply because I am uncertain of not only the alleged entity's origin, but the truth behind the brand.

To put it simply, a destructive person in real life will ultimately be a malevolent person in the afterlife. You don't have to be a demon to be evil, by any definition. A life full of torment and horrible memories will become the ghost, just as a life full of happiness will.

The cases and personal experiences you are about to read cover the gamut. Some are crowded with bereavement, while others are full of wonder. Some are bound with fear, while others are burdened with insanity.

My name is Stephen Lancaster, and I have been involved in the field of paranormal research extensively since 1997. In 1987, I experienced a supernatural occurrence that still to this day I do not understand. A lot has happened over the past few decades that I think you will find frightening, captivating, and thought provoking.

In the beginning, I conducted all of my research alone. I always felt it best to be independent when in the field. I guess in a way it was to insure that I would be the only one accountable for anything that may have occurred. In later years, I would form a paranormal investigation team known as the P.I.T. Crew, comprised of former military, medical practitioners, law enforcement, media professionals, other professionals, and general enthusiasts.

Regardless of good or bad, I want to share this world with you. I want you to see what life is really like living outside the realm of everyday society. I wish for you to see the hardships, the risks, the fulfillment, and the reality.

For some reason paranormal research has always displayed magnetism that continues to draw me and many others in. As you will see, a life absorbed inside a force we have yet to understand can be a dangerous one, both physically and mentally. Ever and again it is wise to walk away from it, for the ghosts never leave. They are always there and this can and will destroy you. We can all fool ourselves into thinking we have it all figured out. I can't even begin to count the times I was confident I had. The afterlife can haunt you and never stop. They call me, they call us, "ghost hunters." But I often wonder what is actually being hunted.

Many people, including you, will read through these pages and question everything. Many of you will not. This may be a little presumptuous to say, but I believe no matter who you are, you are reading this book because of an interest in the afterlife and anything involving the supernatural. Do you believe, or do you wish to believe? I am certain you have asked yourself that at one point or another.

Many people will walk away from these pages with a little more assurance that there is in fact something beyond what is currently known concerning life and death. Many people will have seen nothing more than a series of ghost stories.

Either way, this is a world I have chosen to live in. Whether or not these experiences are full of truth, simply misunderstood, or just plain radical, every story told here actually happened.

So what is this book? It definitely is not a "how to" book and it definitely is not the result of exposure to overly-produced television programming. This book chronicles my experiences and the experiences of many others in dealing with the supernatural. The chapters within reveal many dark and extreme cases that most of you were never aware of.

With every case, I am forced to look at myself, look at the people I work with, and look back at the case before it, completely questioning what I thought I already knew. Retrospectively speaking, these chapters were my thoughts at the time the events transpired. Everything changes.

What once I believed, I shudder to admit I thought so. I look back on certain situations and completely question myself, as I am sure I will do again in the future. This line of work is full of wrong turns and wrong answers. The afterlife became my life. It chewed me up, spit me out, and drove me to the brink of insanity. But there is many a slip between a cup and a lip.

This book is a continuation of my paranormal life story. This is where I am at now. These are testaments of the supernatural, and for some of us they became scars that may one day haunt you too.

ONE

The Fascinating Case of Mrs. Weller

Once in a while I come across an interesting individual with a very captivating, somewhat inconceivable, yet authentic story to tell. The fascinating case of Mrs. Weller was one of those stories. She saw *things* her entire life and had an uncanny ability to speak with complete accuracy of things that had yet to happen.

Most ghost tales start and end the same, with a person falling victim to some crazy and terrible tragedy that later leads them to become the subject of a campfire tale. Not all stories are completely ridiculous, however. Many cases I have conducted as a paranormal researcher did have a rather disturbing factual history to them. When I heard the story about Mrs. Weller, my ears immediately perked up with interest. Her story was completely like nothing I had ever heard before. This was the first time that I heard about paranormal occurrences that happened before they happened. Confused? Read on.

Mrs. Weller died of natural causes in 1991. I would not become privy to her extraordinary story for another nineteen years, however. What makes her story completely intriguing is the fact she predicted everything I am about to tell you, prior to her death.

In 2009, I met her fifty-seven-year-old son, Don Weller. Mr. Weller is an extremely generous, educated, and well-respected man. He is also curiously interesting in his own right. The first few months after we met brought forth little in the conversation department. We had very little in common and there was nearly a thirty-year generational gap between us. Of course, that does not really matter. Our conversations consisted of what most would call "obligatory speak."

Don was retired and looking for some work to occupy his mind and time. Having lost his wife years before, he needed to get out of his house and back around the general public to help cure his loneliness. He found a job at a location I was conducting extensive paranormal research at. I had been investigating this place for nearly one year when Don started working there.

Don was unaware of who I was, and at the time he did not know the haunted history of the location. The paranormal activity in this building was kept low-key and out of the public eye. Even today the location remains anonymous throughout my work, per the request of the building's owner.

For all Don knew, I was just a typical employee at the location. I would see Don first thing in the morning, five days a week. He would often see me coming in and out with various electrical equipment and cameras yet never asked what it was exactly I did. He worked the front area of the building, dealing with the general public. I was mostly floating around doing what I do throughout the building, and rarely spoke to him. The most either one of us had said to each other was, "Hello," or "Good morning," or "Have a good one."

It was not until August of 2010, when Don witnessed something paranormal in the building, that we finally had a reason to start talking a little more than what we had.

He showed up that morning for work right on time, like he always did. I had not seen him the day before, and what he wanted to tell me had happened then. When Don arrived for work he wasted no time asking me if I had experienced anything out of the ordinary in the building.

With coffee in hand, Don proceeded to start the conversation that would later cause us to become great friends. Don asked me if I had witnessed anything strange in the building in the past year. I told him that I did and was curious as to why he would ask me that.

Don showed concern that I would think he was crazy, and I assured him that would not be the case. I almost laughed at the idea, considering the reason I was in the building to begin with.

Referring to a table, Don began to describe the unexplainable occurrence. He said that around two in the afternoon, two pistols on the table came out of their holsters and fell to the floor. At first, he wasn't sure exactly what happened. After hearing something behind him fall, which was the first pistol, he quickly turned around in time to see the second pistol come out of its holster and hit the floor. Don emphasized how dumbfounding and freaky that was to witness. Two pistols, without human intervention, lifted up out of their holsters and landed on the tile below.

I have to admit this raised my curiosity, having seen those pistols lay in the same spot on that table for weeks. Don assured me that he was the only person in the building at the time of the incident. Immediately I thought of the building surveillance system that I lived behind for a year, observing the paranormal phenomena related to my case. He seemed excited that I had access to the surveillance system footage and was eager to find out what exactly I did there.

There were only a handful of people who had keys to the office area where the building's surveillance hard drive was kept. I was one of those people. We entered the office area and I sat down at the desk to start scanning through the previous day's surveillance on the computer, around the time he had mentioned. Sure enough, I found it. The footage revealed exactly what Don had described down to every last detail.

In the video, I could blatantly see Don looking in the direction of the guns in question. There was no audio to the video so it was impossible to confirm the sound of the pistol hitting the floor. The only thing I had was Don's reaction—jerking his head in that direction at the time he claims the first one fell.

Unfortunately, the camera that caught this incident was filming from all the way across the room. The pistols were at least fifty feet from the camera. Even while viewing this in full-screen mode all I could see was something falling to the ground. The image was not large enough to see what that something was. Don, of course, said it was the pistols.

I could tell in the video however that Don did, in fact, pick two things up off of the floor and place them back on the table. I had no reason to believe he was lying, but it was such a shame that was not caught more vividly on the surveillance camera.

Don was convinced a "damn ghost or something" was haunting the facility. At that point, I looked at him and stated that I felt the same way. Don looked at me very curiously. He glanced at me and tilted his head like a dog would when it gives you that confused look. Without hesitation, I pulled up the Internet on the computer, to show him a piece of video previously captured inside the building.

I explained to him that the footage was captured a year prior. I played the footage for the curious Don. His face dropped to an expressionless state, with his eyes as big as saucers. He was leaning over me to be as close as he could to the computer monitor. I could actually smell the coffee he had been drinking moments earlier.

Without saying a word, he turned and walked out of the office. I honestly thought I pushed him to the edge and he was leaving the premises. I often forget how desensitized I am to the paranormal and how sometimes others do not handle images like this too well. A few moments later, Don returned with his reading glasses on and asked to see the incredible footage again.

Don and I ended up watching that particular video about a dozen times. He was not saying much during the viewings other than your typical "Wow" or "What the hell?" After the final viewing, I looked up at him and we just stared at one another for a moment.

I further explained that the footage was captured in the room adjacent to where we were sitting. I played the video one last time and sure enough, at that point he recognized the room. The door to that room was only a few feet from the table the pistols had fallen from behind Don, the day before.

After collecting himself, Don asked me how I had obtained the video to begin with. I told him the truth. The video was sent to me over a year ago. The owner wanted my opinion on it since what was captured in the video happened to be the exact thing his employees had been describing for months. After my brief explanation, Don smiled and said, "a ghost."

I showed Don a few of the other videos I had on my website that were taken from that same location. Don stared in amazement and I felt that was a good point to properly introduce myself. I finally referred to myself as a paranormal researcher and he quickly made sense of why I was there. Don seemed excited to learn his workplace was haunted and that he wasn't, in fact, crazy.

Moments later I took some time to examine the pistols and the surrounding area. My initial thoughts were correct. There was no rational explanation for those pistols unsheathing and falling to the floor. That occurrence remained a mystery but was certainly added to the case file for the location along with Don's testimony.

That day forever changed our relationship. For five days a week we would continue to discuss all things paranormal. Don was always interested to hear about my latest case and findings. Every once in a while he would mention a set of photos he had in his possession that he wanted to show me. I told him each time that I would love to see them.

After his wife died, Don placed a large portion of his belongings in a storage facility, including boxes of old photographs. He would never tell me what the photos were about. Don would simply say, "You're not going to believe it when I show them to you. But I need to show them to you on a day there is time to talk. It's a cool story and I think you will appreciate it."

As time would tell, the day finally came when Don decided to show me the pictures. He had taken the time to dig them out of storage just so he could show me. Don was certain I would be completely interested in them and he was right.

In October 2010, Don arrived at work with a large manila envelope in one hand and his coffee in the other. I knew before he said a word what was in that envelope. He had it written all over his face with that sinister little smirk he often wore. I also expected it.

He had asked me the day before if I could hang out for a little while in the morning to talk. I told him I could. So I kind of figured he was planning on bringing in the photographs and finally telling me his story. The time had come to hear the fascinating case of Mrs. Weller.

Don was aware that I knew what he had in his possession, and before I could say a word, he asked me if I had time to hear the whole story before viewing the pictures. At this point, I was dying of anticipation so of course I agreed.

We walked outside so he could smoke while the story was being told. I sat down on the fire escape stairs as he stood there puffing away on his cigarette and sipping coffee. At first nothing was being said. It was almost like he was emotionally preparing himself before beginning. Don was showing signs of hesitation almost, as if he was second-guessing the idea of telling the story to me.

Since I could tell what Don was about to say bordered on the emotionally deep and dear side of things to him, I decided to break the ice. I wanted him to be comfortable telling me something that was not necessarily scientific in nature. All Don knew of me was how obsessed I was about scientific validation of paranormal occurrences. I was worried he thought my mind was closed off to experiences completely spiritual in nature.

I took that moment to mention the new book I was writing. Don had no idea I was writing about a near dozen of my most productive cases in the paranormal field. After I finished explaining the ins and outs of my book, Don decided to tell me his story.

Mrs. Weller was a very loved, special, and gifted person. She typically kept to herself and never bothered with business outside of her own. Don's mother was never the gossiping type and when she did speak, one could expect nothing but honesty, as hurtful as it may occasionally be.

Mrs. Weller was a very spiritual lady by nature. She was also an exceptional cook. Her favorite room in the house was the kitchen and you did not dare mess with anything in there. That was her territory and no one argued with that. Every day brought forth a new delicious masterpiece for her family to enjoy.

Mrs. Weller also had rare and unique gifts or special skills beyond the norm. She never spoke of them to any of her family except Don, but the rest of them knew. Don's mother never once referred to herself as a psychic, medium, clairvoyant, or anything of the like. She just *knew* things. When she spoke, her family believed it, and every time her suggestion would turn out to be correct. Don believed his mother to be spiritually connected.

Don said on many occasions his mother would tell him stories about the ghosts she talked to. She claimed to have seen and spoken with her father numerous times after his death. Mrs. Weller started having experiences with spirits at a very young age.

Don was never really certain what to say when it came to all of that. He did know his mother was rather sincere about it. The woman never lied and if she claimed to be talking with the dead, who was he to argue? The rest of his family would occasionally try to talk about what they thought was going on with his mother, but Don always kept the things she told him secret.

His family often suggested she was a psychic or a medium. Mrs. Weller looked out for everyone and would always lend her advice. It was not rare for her to call a family member to warn them about something. Of course, that something would occur as she suggested. This led many of Don's family to believe in Mrs. Weller's secret gift.

The part of her story Don focused on was the last week of her life. He insisted that there was no way in hell his mother could have known such things without some form of spiritual or supernatural connection. He certainly had my attention so far with the story. I could tell he was bringing out old emotions and this was difficult for him to do. He loved his mother dearly.

As he continued, his eyes started glazing over while he was staring off at nothing. Don was definitely fighting to hold back the tears and I did not pressure him. I simply waited for him to pick up where he left off in the story. There were many pauses in his speech. Thinking about his mother, and telling this story for the first time, was really taking an emotional toll on him.

Before her death, she had spoken with Don about a couple of very important things that were going to happen after she died. He told me that his mother had predicted her own death right down to the day, and that was not all. Don emphasized that the events of that week, and the ones that followed her death, were embedded into his brain.

On November 6, 1991, Don was in Seattle, Washington, as a speaker for a week-long business convention. About halfway through the week he received a phone call from his mother. She was advising him to return home as soon as possible. He stressed to her that leaving the conference early would place a lot a pressure on his partner to finish out the week. But Mrs. Weller was adamant about getting her son back to his home in Savannah, Georgia, promptly.

Don could tell his mother was very serious and he made the proper arrangements to return home as quickly as he could. His partner understood and was willing to finish out the conference alone. Don caught the first flight out of Seattle that evening.

He arrived back in Savannah early the next day and caught a taxi to his childhood home. Mrs. Weller was waiting and had yet another delicious meal ready for him. As soon as Don entered her house he was instructed to have a seat at the kitchen table and eat what she had prepared for him.

Mrs. Weller joined him at the table but sat in silence until Don was finished with his meal. The whole time he was eating all he wanted to do was find out what was so important that he had to fly across the country immediately to see her. Don expected the worst. He expected to hear his mother had developed cancer or some other terminal illness.

Every time he would attempt to get her to speak she would simply tell him to finish his meal. Don respected his mother's wishes and finished eating what she had cooked.

Mrs. Weller cleaned up the table and sat back down across from her son. As sincerely as she could, Mrs. Weller told her son that she would not be around much longer. Don of course suggested a terminal illness. She explained to him that her health was not going to be the cause of death. Mrs. Weller was completely healthy.

She told her thirty-eight-year-old son that her life would end in a week. Don of course said what any loving son would say and told her to quit speaking such nonsense. She raised her voice and said that he knew she was never wrong about this kind of thing. Don agreed and respected her adamancy.

Mrs. Weller stood up and walked across the kitchen. She opened a drawer typically used for storing mail and pulled out an envelope. She told her son that this had been written only a few hours before he arrived home. The envelope was sealed with "Do not open until November 14, 1991," written on the front. That was seven days away.

Mrs. Weller continued by explaining to Don a few occurrences that would take place after her death. She told him that it was of vital importance that he appeared at the church during her funeral. Of course, this was really hard for Don to listen to, yet alone understand. There he sat while his mother was stating she was going to die in seven days, and speaking as if she was already dead.

Don remained sitting, however, and continued listening to every word his mother had to say. Mrs. Weller handed him the envelope with strict instructions not to open it until the day she died. He agreed. She continued by saying that everything he was being told today had also been written down on a piece of paper inside the envelope, to ensure he did not forget.

As the conversation progressed, she told Don that his father would remarry six months after her death. Once again Don tried to talk some sense into her, stating that was crazy talk. Mrs. Weller insisted that she would be correct. His father was going to marry the bimbo secretary that used to work for him over two decades ago. Don sat in disbelief and told his mother that his father's old secretary had moved to California twenty years ago. Mrs. Weller quickly shut him up and said, "I will be right."

Don stopped telling the story and explained to me that his mother never did like her husband's old secretary. She would often refer to her as the "dumb, blonde bimbo." She was around Don's present age of fifty-seven, which made her about twenty years younger than his father.

After educating me on the "dumb, blonde bimbo," Don continued with the story. He told me his mother said she was going to haunt her husband's new wife after she died. He said as she was telling him this, her hand was in the air as if saying, "Stop." She knew Don would want to say something about that and was making sure he just listened and kept his mouth shut. She simply said, "I'm just going to mess with her a little, Donald. I'm just going to mess with her."

After informing Don that his father would remarry and that she was going to haunt his new wife, she once again mentioned the importance of his appearance at the church on the day of her funeral. Don assured her that he would be there.

Mrs. Weller also mentioned his grandmother. She told him to look out for her and to have her at the house often. Don agreed that he would. His grandmother, who was Mrs. Weller's mother, suffered from Alzheimer's disease. Sadly, she would never come to realize her own daughter's death since the inability of acquiring new memories was the main effect of the disease.

After Mrs. Weller had told her son everything she wanted to say, Don gave her a big hug and caught the next plane back to Seattle. He did not want to believe all of the things she had told him. But he knew he had to. This was not the first time his mother had predicted such things and was right about them.

Seven days later, Don received the phone call that his mother had passed away of natural causes. Once again he caught a plane back to Savannah to help with the funeral arrangements and to be with his family. Upon arriving back at his childhood home, he opened the letter his mother had given him seven days prior.

Don stopped telling me the story. He reached into his back pocket and pulled out a folded-over envelope. The envelope showed age and was full of creases. Don had held on to this letter for nearly twenty years. He handed me the letter and gave me permission to read it.

I have to admit the strangest feeling overcame me. I've listened to hundreds of people tell me their stories over the years. Sometimes those stories hit home while other times I completely find myself indifferent to them.

But hearing the way Don spoke about his mother really captured my heart. I pictured him sitting in an old rocking chair in front of a fireplace puffing on cigarettes and telling his story. The man had a gift just like his mother, in a way.

I glanced down at the envelope in my hand. To be honest, I wanted to find a reason not to believe his story. I guess that's just my nature. But so far his words and this aged envelope told me otherwise. The story so far was resonating deeply inside, as if I were connected to it on a personal level.

Don interrupted my daydreaming, urging me to open the letter and read his mother's words. I looked up at him and then back down to the envelope.

The letter was dated November 7, 1991, which was the exact date his mother told him she had a week to live.

November 7, 1991

Dear Donald,

I want you to be joyous on this day, my dear son. Do not mourn my death for now I sit beside God. I want you to smile today knowing that I will forever be beside you. Anytime you wish to speak with me you know where to find me. I will be in my favorite room.

There are some things I wish you to know, Donald. We have already spoken about those things, so I'm writing this as a reminder so you don't forget. You now know that I was not wrong about my death and there are a few things to come I do not want you to forget.

Your father is going to remarry and it will be to that bimbo blonde. I was not joking when I said I was going to have some fun with her after I died. You will know it is me because I will be in my favorite room. Don't worry darling, I am just going to mess with her for a little while.

It is also important that you be at the church on the day of my funeral. You won't know why at first, but the answer will present itself soon. It is very important, Donnie! Also, take care of your grandmother. I fear her illness strengthens.

Always with you,
Mom

P.S. Don't forget to smile!

As I sat on the fire escape reading this letter, Don remained quiet as he continued smoking cigarettes. When I finished reading the letter I handed it back to him without saying a word. I mean, what do you say to that? This was a really personal thing for Don to share with me. Although I really appreciated it, I did feel somewhat awkward about the whole thing.

I felt as if I was reading a letter from the dead, and I guess I was. Although I knew his mother had written it prior to passing away, there was still an unsettling quality to it.

Don immediately asked me how I felt about his story so far. I did not know what to say at this point, so I simply asked if his father did in fact marry the, ahem, "bimbo."

Don continued on with the story by telling me that his father did in fact remarry and it was to the "dumb, blonde bimbo" secretary. His father traveled a lot due to his occupation and I could not help but think that he was most likely having an affair all those years and Don's mother knew it. But that is just me attempting to rationally explain the situation. I did not say that out loud however.

Jokingly I suggested to Don that this would be the perfect point to tell me his mother haunted the woman. As you can expect, it was confirmed.

Don's stepmother moved into their old house, of course, and it was not long after doing so that she started to experience strange and unexplainable occurrences. Don vividly recalled the day his stepmother mentioned the weird happenings around the house.

It was summer of 1992, and Don was back in town for his father's birthday. His father and new wife had been married for a few months at this point. Don was planning on spending a few weeks in his childhood home to be with his father and to possibly get to know his stepmother a little bit better. Don admitted it was quite difficult to fully accept her, especially considering she was two years younger than he was.

After a few nights of staying in his old home, Don started to notice peculiar things happening in the kitchen. One night in particular, the kitchen light refused to turn off. At first he thought this was most likely a faulty switch. But then his stepmother entered the room and the kitchen light exploded into a million pieces. Don and his stepmother cleaned up the mess and replaced the bulb. The kitchen light worked fine the rest of the night.

The next morning, Don entered the kitchen to make everyone breakfast. He was surprised to see that every cabinet door and drawer was open. He closed everything back up before anybody else could see it. Don made breakfast as planned and his father and stepmother soon joined him in the kitchen.

While they were eating breakfast, Don decided to ask his father and stepmother if they had experienced anything weird in the house. His father laughed in disbelief while his stepmother jumped at the chance to share her stories.

His stepmother said that ever since she moved into the home, strange events had been taking place in the kitchen. She suggested that it happened so often it was easily predicted.

She continued by saying that nearly every night sounds were vividly originating from the kitchen. Like Don, his stepmother experienced the cabinet doors and drawers opening.

Don stopped telling me the story for a moment to point out that he had experienced the cabinet doors and drawers as well, before his stepmother had ever mentioned it. He told me that he knew it was his mother. The kitchen was her favorite room and she would be damned to allow some other woman cook for her husband. I acknowledged what he was telling me, and Don continued.

His stepmother claimed she could never cook anything to completion because something in the kitchen would not allow her. Don's father thought this was all complete nonsense and began laughing at her stories.

However, both Don and his stepmother witnessed the exploding light bulb. Upon her entrance into the kitchen the light blew up. Mr. Weller, Sr., kept laughing and among his giggles he mumbled that is was probably his late wife.

Even though his new wife was now yelling at him about the cabinet doors and lights flickering and exploding, he assured his son and her that there was no such thing as ghosts. Don knew better, however. He knew that his mother was keeping her word. She was just "messing with her for a little bit." His father never talked about stuff like that. He would always blow off the stories revolving around the supernatural. Don believed that his father knew it was his late wife. He was not going to admit it, however.

The following week, Don kept the promise to his mother and flew his grandmother Loraine in from Michigan to spend some time with them. His father and stepmother prepared their bedroom for her to stay in, while they slept on the pull-out couch in the living room.

That evening they all sat around the dinner table in the kitchen mostly talking about Don's career. His grandmother never asked one time about who the blonde woman was. Don believed she thought it was his girlfriend or wife and never said anything since they were about the same age. Out of respect, his father and stepmother agreed to keep their hands off of one another while his late wife's mother was staying with them.

Loraine also never asked where her daughter was. Don assumed she figured her daughter was out shopping or at work. Although his grandmother had been at the funeral, the disease prevented her from remembering that.

Dinner came and went and his grandmother was soon off to bed. A few hours later, Don and the rest of his family turned in for the night. The next morning, Don's stepmother thought she would attempt to make everyone breakfast. She went to grab the skillet that was sitting on the stove and ended up burning her hand to blisters. She screamed and dropped the skillet on the kitchen floor. Don and his father raced into the kitchen to see what all the commotion was about. She claimed the stove had been left on and the skillet had sat there hot as fire. Don and his father stated that neither one of them placed a skillet on the stove at any time since last night.

Don's father had prepared dinner the night before, but the entire family, including his stepmother, cleaned up everything. She suggested that possibly Loraine had started cooking something and forgot about it. Both Don and his father completely dismissed that since she would have walked past them to get to the kitchen.

After Don and his father tended to her burn, they teamed up and made everybody a full breakfast. Once the table was set, Don's grandmother entered the kitchen and sat down at the table.

Not that she would have remembered anyway, Don asked her if she cooked anything in the kitchen late last night. His grandmother said that she had never left her room. The four of them sat at the table and began eating breakfast. The room was quiet until Loraine decided to speak up. Conversation over breakfast was certainly one for the books.

Don's grandmother suggested that she had "the most wonderful conversation" with his recently deceased mother the night before. However, if you need reminding, his mother was now dead. Mr. Weller, Sr., attempted to interrupt the conversation and explain to Loraine that her daughter had passed away, but Don prevented him from saying a word.

Loraine continued by saying that they talked all of the time and that her daughter came to see her last week. Don knew that was impossible.

His grandmother also said that she knew he would be coming to pick her up. She knew he would be bringing her to Savannah, because his mother told her so. Loraine joked with Don, claiming his mother said he would forget.

Don did not forget. He just did not know what to say to his grandmother. There sat his grandmother claiming to not only have spoken with his late mother the previous night, but also the previous week back in Michigan. I can only imagine what must have been going on in Don's mind at that moment.

Don told me that his grandmother stayed with them for about a week before catching a plane back to Michigan. His father dismissed everything she had said as being a direct result of the Alzheimer's disease. Don, however, knew there was a good possibility everything his grandmother said was true.

So far into his story, all I could say to Don was that his mother was right about everything. He enjoyed hearing that from me and once again said that she *knew* things.

The skillet incident was the last time anything out of the ordinary occurred in Don's childhood home. It was almost like Don's mother was just giving his stepmother one last jab before calling it quits. She had kept her promise and only "messed with her a little."

I told Don that his story was absolutely fascinating. I found myself so engrossed in his storytelling that I nearly forgot about the photographs he wanted me to see. To be honest, I was completely satisfied with what he had told me so far.

This wasn't exactly something I could personally validate and to be frank, I really didn't care to. Not all personal experiences can be proven. They are what they are.

As we walked back into the building, Don continued by reminding me that his mother was adamant about his attendance at the funeral. We walked behind the counter and he grabbed the manila envelope and pulled out six photographs. Don handed them to me and I started looking through them. The pictures were taken on the steps of the church immediately following his mother's viewing. They were of Don and some of his family. Immediately I noticed an anomaly in the first photograph. I looked up at Don and laughed.

Of course, he asked me what I was laughing at. I described exactly what I had seen which was what appeared to be a halo over his head. It was interesting to note that he was the only one in the picture with a tilted white circle just above the head. I examined the photograph closely for any sign of lens flare to possibly explain the photographic anomaly. I did not see anything that could explain the image. Don suggested that I take a look at the next picture.

I sat the first photograph on the counter and started looking at the second. Immediately, I noticed the same tilted white circle was still just above Don's head. I was really baffled at this point. It was easy to see that the photographer had moved slightly to the right for this second shot. The family was still standing on the steps in front of the church, but this second picture was shot at a different angle.

I quickly started glancing over the remaining four pictures. Every one of them had the same photographic anomaly just about his head. The really interesting part was that the final three pictures were taken inside the church. There I sat staring at six different pictures. Three pictures taken outside in front of the church and three pictures taken inside the church all showed a halo over Don's head. The same people were the subject of every shot with the exception of one.

Don immediately wanted my thoughts on the subject. I explained to him that I wasn't much of a religious man. However, the only word that came to mind to describe these images was "angelic."

Don asked me to take another look at the photographs while he used the restroom. I could tell by the way he asked me that there was something else to be seen.

While he was gone, I sat there examining the six photographs further. I saw nothing else out of the ordinary to comment on. Don returned after a few minutes and we continued discussing the photographs.

He immediately asked if I noticed anything else bizarre in any of the photographs. I honestly had to tell him I had not.

Since I was apparently missing the obvious, Don went ahead and singled out a particular individual in one of the photographs.

Still confused, I told him all I could see were members of his family.

Don grabbed the first photograph taken outside on the church steps and pointed out each person to me. There were eleven people total in the photograph.

He then handed me one of the pictures taken inside the church and there was one extra person in that one. The other five pictures had eleven people in them. This picture however, had twelve.

I admitted to seeing the extra person in the picture, so I asked Don who it was.

Don reached into his back pocket and pulled out his wallet. He opened it up to reveal a photograph of his mother. On the back of the photograph was her full name along with the date. The picture from his wallet was of his mother in 1989 just two years prior to her death.

In total amazement I completely acknowledged the fact that the extra person in the photograph looked just like his mother.

I immediately questioned the timing of the pictures and suggested the images were taken prior to the funeral.

Don corrected me and said the pictures were in fact taken the day of his mother's funeral. He followed that up with a sinister, sly grin and said, "I told you these pictures were amazing."

I sat there for a few more minutes examining those photographs. The woman in the picture really looked like she was standing right beside Don. She was not faint in her appearance like most photographs claiming to have a ghost in them. If Don had never pointed her out, I would have been left to assume she was just another member of his family attending the funeral.

I instantly thanked Don for sharing such an amazing and personal story with me.

He said it has been nearly twenty years since he last viewed the photographs. Don didn't care whether or not I believed his story. He was just happy to tell it.

I had no reason to think his story was bogus. I found it all very interesting. Between the letter, the photographs and everything else he told me, I think his mother had some sort of spiritual connection that was—and still is—unexplainable.

I jokingly told Don that I refused to believe he was an angel despite the halo in the photographs. He said that it was a sign his mother would always be watching over him.

Don said his father had seen the photographs, yet never said a word about his late wife being seen in one of them. Don said he believed his father to have known she was there but decided to keep that fact to himself.

I couldn't help but ask Don if I could include his story in a future book. In a comedic fashion he agreed, as long as I referred to his stepmother as a "dumb, blonde bimbo." He said his reasoning behind that was simply to make his mother smile.

That isn't necessarily something I would do, but it's what the man wanted.

Don and I parted ways. I returned to my office and immediately started writing down the bulk of what he had just told me. I was pleased to hear him grant permission to include this story in a future book about the supernatural. The story of Mrs. Weller certainly fits comfortably in that category.

I have heard my share of psychic tales and premonitions, but nothing quite as concrete as this. I can honestly say I have never heard of a person predicting their own death with such accuracy, and then on top of that predicting a haunting for which they are responsible. How could this woman have known the exact day of her death? She died of natural causes. This was all extraordinary.

Those photographs were truly amazing as well. The pictures alone would be meaningless without the story to back it all up. Mrs. Weller knew something was going to come of those pictures. She was so intent on making sure her son would be at the church. The very last thing she said in her letter pointed straight to the photographs: "Don't forget to smile!"

Years after Don shared his story with me, individuals who were a part of his mother's life came forward with their encounters involving the ghost of Mrs. Weller.

Personally, I expected it from family members, but when people who had never met her started writing me with ghostly tales, my interest in the case peaked once again.

I always hold more credence in paranormal claims from those who had no prior knowledge of the stories. One in particular came from Martha Springfield, who relocated to Georgia in 2012.

She e-mailed me after allegedly witnessing Mrs. Weller sitting in the pews of the church in broad daylight, in the middle of the week.

Martha walked into the church on a Tuesday afternoon to ask God for help with a sick relative. As she was praying, a somber and gentle female voice was heard to her left. That voice said, "He will help you and if he can't, believe in his reason."

Martha believed she was alone in the church that day. When she opened her eyes from prayer and glanced to the side of her, an elderly lady with a welcoming smile was sitting next to her.

Martha's attention turned quickly from the mysterious woman to Reverend William Miller. The reverend was concerned after finding Martha sobbing in the pews.

Martha, however, had no recollection of crying and assured him that another woman, moments earlier, was sitting beside her.

Reverend Miller questioned Martha's claims, stating that no other person was in the church.

The following Sunday, Martha attended mass. She started asking around and describing the woman she had seen. It did not take long for her to learn the story of Mrs. Weller from other church members.

She attempted to contact numerous family members in hopes of hearing more about her. Martha was able to contact Don Weller, who eventually referred her to me.

I found it so interesting that a woman from out of town described Mrs. Weller in great detail, without any prior knowledge of her life, her death, the haunting, and her amazing predictions.

Martha's bizarre and unique tale was not the end of the supernatural claims.

Don's father passed away years ago. He left the house to Don's stepmother. In less than a year of living alone in the home, his stepmother sold the property. She claimed that the paranormal activity returned following her husband's death.

Mrs. Weller is still in the kitchen.

TWO

Eidolon Fields

Stepping on the grounds of Eidolon Fields is the closest any human being will ever get to hell and still have a heartbeat.

That may sound a bit overdramatic, but a weekend on the property nearly took my life and the lives of my colleagues.

We were chased out of the woods and into the fields by a pack of hyenas, unloaded clips of ammunition at something that was apparently impossible to hit, fought dehydration in 120-degree weather, survived being attacked and knocked down stairs, and walked away with some of the best evidence ever documented in favor of the supernatural.

In fact, A&E Biography filmed a segment streamlining the horrific events that took place that weekend, for a show entitled *My Ghost Story*. A great deal of the evidence gathered during my research at the Eidolon Fields can be viewed during that particular segment.

The weekend of August 5, 2011, proved to be a monumental series of days that stretched both our physical and mental abilities. We traveled to Warsaw, North Carolina, to spend three days on an eighty-five-acre former plantation, at the request of the new owner of the property.

Mr. Scotts purchased the property only a few months prior to contacting us. His dream was to completely renovate the rundown and overgrown location and bring it back to the original form as it stood in 1840.

Unfortunately, Mr. Scotts purchased more than an 85-acre property with three barely standing slave quarters and a rundown plantation house. Unfortunately, Mr. Scotts would never see his dream of renovating the property come to life. Mr. Scotts purchased Eidolon Fields and it was not long before he realized exactly what that meant.

The strange phenomena he started experiencing while on the property prompted him to contact my paranormal investigation team and me. Mr. Scotts was hearing phantom voices in the plantation house, witnessing bizarre lights across the old soybean fields, and on a few occasions believed he saw otherworldly figures, both inside and outside the historic home.

The discovery of human-like footprints and what appeared to be claw marks burned into the ceiling of the attic was enough to push Mr. Scotts into seeking outside assistance to hopefully help answer his questions about these experiences.

I assembled a group of six from my paranormal team, the P.I.T. Crew, and a German Shepherd named Kai. The team of six consisted of Allen Bess, former military; Noelle Harper, a private investigator; Spencer Holland, a teacher; Valere Bilichka, a nurse; Jeff Miller, law enforcement; and of course me, the published author. Every individual on this case had a strong background in paranormal research, and frankly I needed the best I had ever worked with to even consider tackling something of this scale and nature.

Upon arriving in Warsaw, I discovered the main plantation house was easy to find. The historic building stood proud on the edge of the property line.

We arrived at the location at four o'clock in the afternoon on Friday, August 11. The owner had hidden the key to the plantation house for us to use for access to the building. The property was ours for the weekend, and I think it spoke volumes that he would not step foot on the property to at least get us started.

The weekend ahead was going to be extremely challenging for all of us. The intense heat forced us to bring a crate of bottled water. The elements were working against us and in addition to that, the plantation house did not have running water or electricity. Knowing this ahead of time really helped us prepare for a weekend that required our equipment to have enough stored power to last three days.

The team and I were roughing it for the weekend, so to speak. A case like this is a rarity, when considering the preparation, environment, and physical demands.

With only about five hours of solid daylight remaining, I decided to organize the team for a reconnaissance mission to survey the entire property. We needed to determine the best placement for night vision cameras and our base camp, and just acquire general knowledge of the land. The team and I also needed to locate the three mentioned slave quarters.

The entire group was present except the team's tech manager, Jeff Miller. He was in the middle of picking up and transporting our base of operations equipment trailer and all-terrain vehicles. The all-terrain vehicles, or ATVs, were to aid us when travelling over and through the rough terrain.

I had no time to wait for his arrival. We quickly unloaded a few of the crates containing firearms, tracking equipment, and water. Backpacks were loaded with as much water as they would carry, firearms were checked, and tracking equipment was packed away in our vests.

With the team ready to move, arms detail began.

P.I.T. Crew head investigator, Allen Bess, briefed the team on the arms detail for safety, awareness, and to emphasize the dangerous situations we could possibly encounter. His military background was essential to certain elements of this case.

While Allen was briefing the team on the reconnaissance mission, I was prepping a Canon GL-2 film camera to begin documenting the weekend. This would prove to be a huge handicap for me, considering that on one arm I had a twelve-gauge shotgun and on the other a $3,000 video camera.

Not only was I required to be alert for whatever the environment could throw at us, I also needed to be attentive to what I was filming.

Allen finished the briefing, and armed with pistols, shotguns, and various pieces of tracking equipment, we began our trek across the old, forgotten fields.

Even at five in the afternoon, the summer sun beating down on us was extremely brutal. It took us about twenty minutes to reach the edge of the fields where the thick wooded area began. The woods were believed to be the location of the slave quarters. Little did I know then, that we would discover a whole lot more than that.

The five of us stood at the edge of the field, completely drenched in sweat. I stared back across the field and I could barely see the plantation house from the distance we had traveled.

Before entering the woods, Allen gave brief and stern instructions on the reconnaissance mission. Allen would take point, which simply means to be at the head of the group. Per my suggestion and for documentation purposes, I requested to cover the rear of the group. That placed the three women on the team in the middle, and protected by firearms from whatever awaited within the trees.

Not long after we entered the woods, the first slave quarters were discovered. Near the slave quarters was a second structure, which we determined to be an old tobacco house.

Both structures were still well intact, despite their age and lack of care. Various ropes, tied into shapes most commonly used to represent Voodoo, hung from doorways and windowsills. This was not uncommon, considering many of the former slaves practiced Voodoo.

The rope symbols were meant to warn and scare off potential physical and spiritual danger. The shape of a snake appeared to be the one most commonly used in this situation.

After exploring and documenting the two buildings we pressed deeper into the woods. The time was now eight o'clock and daylight was slowly welcoming nightfall.

This was of huge concern to me. We had yet to discover the remaining two slave quarters. Finding ourselves caught in the darkness of night surrounded by thick forest, in an area unfamiliar to us, was not exactly a pleasant thought.

Against better judgment, we decided to continue on. Before doing so, we equipped ourselves with headlamps, flashlights, and glow sticks. All cameras documenting the reconnaissance mission were switched over to night vision.

I activated and placed a glow stick on the ground where we were standing as a visual marker. We pressed on.

About an hour later we stumbled upon a skeleton of what appeared to be some kind of canine. The bones were nearly all present and still intact, which is a rare thing to find in the woods. Most of the time random predators will rip a piece of a carcass off and carry it away. This was different.

Not an ounce of flesh remained on the skeleton, which meant it had been in that spot and left alone for a very long time. The bones showed no signs of an attack or damage from a man-made device.

The skull of the animal was easily the most intriguing aspect. Four fangs, each about an inch and a half long, were the focal point of the jaw. With two fangs on top and two on the bottom, even dead this animal had a very menacing and intimidating appearance.

We packed up the entire skeleton, piece by piece, and returned to searching the woods for the remaining slave quarters.

As the team kept walking, whispers asking more about what we just found only added to the creepiness of the situation. I was curious, too. I mean, I was the one carrying the bones of an animal no other creature would even eat. Granted, animals are perceptive and disease could have been the cause of death. That would have certainly been a logical conclusion to explore and possibly explain why nothing ate it.

About fifteen minutes later, we found a small pond nestled within a wall of trees. This seemed like a good place to stop and give the team a chance to rest, and to allow Kai some much needed water.

Although the sun was no longer above us, the humidity was just as unbearable. I logged ninety-eight degrees Fahrenheit at ten o' clock, on the ambient thermometer attached to my vest.

As we stood close to the edge of the pond, watching Kai splash around in the water and talking softly amongst one another, P.I.T. Crew case manager Valere Bilichka quickly silenced all of us, after hearing something peculiar.

Valere had the team's full attention when she described hearing laughter just beyond the trees lining the pond. We were all silently looking, filming, and shining lights in the direction she was pointing, when suddenly very vivid laughter came from behind us. We all heard it that time.

Allen and I turned around and quickly loaded bullets into the chambers of our firearms. I handed my video camera off to Spencer. We heard nothing moving through the woods while we were standing there in silence, yet whatever Valere heard laughing had somehow managed to get completely around us.

The laughing was like nothing any of us had ever heard before in the woods of North Carolina. The laughing also sounded inhuman.

We started whispering to each other about the laughter in an attempt to determine who or what was laughing and more importantly, why. As conversation softly continued, the laughing persisted, only this time it was coming from the right of us, over and across the pond.

Once again, we could see nothing other than trees and mosquitoes that looked like they were straight out of the Jurassic era.

At this stage, we really needed to make a move. On three different occasions we heard laughter seemingly coming from three different directions.

Allen decided to scout out the area we heard the most recent laugh come from. I remained back with the team in case we were dealing with an animal that decided to get a little too friendly.

My head investigator disappeared into the trees, as he went searching for a source of the laughter. At that moment I received a radio transmission from Jeff. He had arrived at the plantation with the remainder of our gear and supplies.

I instructed him to stand-by. As soon as Allen returned, I was planning on pulling us out of the woods for the evening. Something just wasn't sitting right with me, and I could tell the team was anxious to get the hell out of there.

Before we knew it, Allen surfaced from the thick brush, with an intense look on his face. He started speaking loudly as he approached us, instructing the team to move. He kept emphasizing over and over that it was time for us to go.

I asked him what happened, and he described witnessing a pair of self-illuminating eyes peering at him through some brush. He was in total blackout as not to give away his location. Yet, the eyes he saw appeared to be glowing.

Allen described the eyes as being about two-and-a-half feet off the ground. We were all convinced he saw some sort of animal.

Regardless, the experience spooked an armed Allen enough to order the team out of the woods as soon as possible.

The entire team started slowly backing out from the pond area when the laughter was heard once more. I instructed the team to start moving faster.

We continued away from the pond and through the woods in a straight line. Like before, Allen took point and I covered the rear. The entire team was double stepping. There was a lot of nervousness and stress in every one of us.

A crunching sound to the left caught my attention. The sound was similar to when a person steps on a dry stick and snaps it. As I turned to look, the light on my head caught a glimpse of another set of eyes. This time, the eyes were moving right along with every step we took.

Just as Allen described, the eyes were over two feet off the ground.

I yelled up the line to get Allen's attention. He quickly fell back to meet up with me. I described to him what I had just witnessed. I told Allen that whatever this animal was, it was now stalking us. I also entertained the possibility that there was more than one.

With that in mind, I pulled a device out of my vest called a Heatseeker. This device is mostly used by hunters to track wildlife. The Heatseeker does exactly what the name suggests: it seeks heat. With a nine-hundred-foot range, panning the laser through the trees would detect anything that had a heartbeat.

Nearly instantly, the device was registering life forms in every direction. We were completely surrounded by animals. I looked at Allen and the only words that would come out of my mouth were, "Oh shit."

Allen turned around and quickly informed the team of the situation, and without hesitation, we continued on the path to exiting the woods. Meanwhile, I could still see those eyes watching our every move.

Kai started acting very strangely. He was whimpering and pulling on his leash extremely hard. Valere was literally being dragged along behind him. It was taking all of her strength just to hang on to the leash. Kai was not stupid. He knew we were surrounded and being stalked by something, and he sensed it.

Having a German Shepherd run the opposite direction was not a comforting feeling at all. I grabbed my radio and made contact with Jeff, who was awaiting our return in front of the plantation house. I asked Jeff to bring an ATV across the soybean fields and meet us at the edge of the woods. My plan was to have Jeff escort half of the team across the fields and back to safety.

I could see the glow stick I placed on the ground hours earlier just up ahead. That told me we were not very far from the fields. This was a good thing.

In no time, we reached the clearing and were standing at the edge of the fields. I could hear an ATV in the distance, but we weren't out of hot water just yet.

Allen and I kept close watch on the woods behind us, while the rest of the team kept their eyes on the field awaiting Jeff and the transport. We could see multiple sets of glowing eyes about fifty yards into the woods. Those little bastards had stalked us all the way to the field. It turned out we were right about their being more than one.

This was a pack of something, and at that moment, not knowing exactly what wanted to eat us was more frightening than anything else. My heart was nearly jumping out of my chest as my finger was placed firmly on the trigger of the shotgun. I was preparing for the worst-case scenario, while I was questioning in my own head as to why I took this case to begin with.

As Allen and I stood armed and ready for a full-blown animal attack, Jeff arrived with the transport to pick up the team.

The three unarmed investigators, along with Kai, were loaded onto the ATV. I strapped the shotgun to my back and took the camera off of Spencer before they drove off. Allen kept his gun up and ready and aimed into the woods while our four investigators sped off to safety.

Allen and I waited until they were clear of the fields before we started our trek back to the plantation house. Jeff called me on the radio once they arrived.

I was certain this pack of animals would never follow Allen and me into the field. They would lose the cover and protection of the trees and become very vulnerable. From what I had witnessed so far, these animals were intelligent and made sure they had the upper hand.

We had only traveled about a quarter of the way through the dead soybean field, when I was rattled instantly by the sight of two glowing eyes in the field behind us. Allen started yelling at me to explain what I was so excited about.

By the time I could say anything, the eyes were gone. The animal had ducked for cover underneath the leaves of the dead soybeans. I explained to Allen that one of the animals was now in the field coming toward us.

At that moment three more sets of eyes appeared scattered throughout the field. This pack was crouching and using the cover of the soybeans to move through the field undetected. They would disappear in one location then reappear in another and each time draw closer and closer to us.

With urgency in his voice, Allen requested permission to fire off a warning shot at these things in hopes of frightening them away. I wasted no time authorizing that request.

Allen fired in the direction of the animals. The sound of gunfire was easily heard back at the plantation house. Just a few moments later, Jeff was on the radio to me again, to check and see if we were all right. Considering the circumstances, I ignored his call.

The field grew calm for a moment, and both Allen and I felt as if the threat was over. My ears were ringing from the single gunshot. Unfortunately, the gunfire had no real effect on our assailants. Once again, eyes started popping up everywhere.

I thought my heart was going to beat right out of my chest. I felt like I was standing at the gates of hell.

All of a sudden, the sound of an ATV at high speed was heard. Jeff appeared with intentions of hauling us back to the plantation house. Without hesitation, Allen and I screamed at Jeff to turn around. The last thing we wanted was this pack of hungry animals following us back to the house where the rest of the team waited.

With our lives at stake and the threat becoming higher yet, I ordered a full-blown open fire on the animals. Allen and I unloaded every bit of ammunition we had on us at that time. A thick cloud of gunsmoke blanketed the field during the aftermath.

Since we were out of ammunition, I strapped the shotgun to my back and Allen did the same with his rifle. I was really hoping we retaliated enough to prevent them from following us any further because at this point we were completely helpless.

I pulled out a thermal imaging camera from my pack to survey the fields to see if there were any signs of life remaining. Allen stood behind me looking at the screen of the camera as I panned slowly across the field.

Something extraordinary caught our attention nearly simultaneously. We were looking at five figures standing in the field, all giving off body heat on the thermal camera. We both reacted accordingly, by questioning what it was exactly we were looking at.

I looked up from the thermal camera and in the direction it was pointing, and saw nothing. We both shined flashlights in that area. Nobody was there. Yet when we would bring up the thermal camera, five figures were standing there.

Completely astounded at what we were witnessing, and finally glad that something potentially supernatural was occurring, I suggested we return to the plantation house as soon as possible.

Allen and I walked backward the remainder of the trip all the while watching the screen of the thermal imaging camera. The five figures remained standing still. I turned my head to take a quick glance at the direction we were walking, and when I looked back at the camera, the figures were gone.

We arrived back at base camp to find the team eagerly awaiting our return. I walked passed them all with a blank stare, completely ignoring their questions. I continued on to my truck where I had a cooler of water in the back. I stood there drinking and drenching myself in the water.

Due to the exhaustion, I felt as if all but 2 percent of my life had been sucked right out of me. I collapsed to the ground from the heat and exhaustion and landed on my back. I stared at the night sky, pondering the recent events and what we had documented.

What species was the skeleton we found? What was laughing at us in the woods? What stalked us out of the woods? What exactly were those figures caught on the thermal camera? They stood and appeared to be human, yet the naked eye was unable to see them. Was any of this supernatural?

Were those dog-like creatures hounds from hell? Were they shape shifters? Demons? Whatever they were, within seconds we went from fighting off a pack of some sort of creatures, to filming humanoids on a thermal camera, who apparently weren't there.

After lying on the ground for about twenty minutes, I stood up and dusted myself off. I stared silently at my team, who were sitting about fifty feet away in a circle discussing everything that had happened thus far. As I was looking at them, I realized we all had placed our lives in danger and we still had two more days at this location.

We survived the woods, but failed to locate the two remaining slave quarters. It was not a complete loss however. The skeleton, the personal experiences, and the thermal footage proved to weigh heavy on my mind.

Tomorrow we would visit the woods once more, only this time we would have a day's worth of sun to guide us. The sun would be a fortunate and unfortunate element—but certainly a necessary evil.

In daylight, I was hoping to discover the remaining two slave quarters, as well as hopefully locating a carcass or two from our intense evening of firing off dozens of bullets at would-be assailants.

We still had the house to search as well, and that was set for Saturday evening after we spent the day on a second reconnaissance mission through the woods.

I approached the team to find them all on their cell phones, browsing the Internet, desperately trying to find an image and species that matched the skeleton we found. I could tell the team was sitting uneasy over all the unanswered questions.

Allen requested I take a look at an image he had pulled up on his phone. We walked away from the others and kneeled down by the skeleton. Allen placed his phone with the image next to the skull lying in the grass.

Sure enough, the image he had pulled looked disturbingly similar to the skull on the ground. The image he had pulled up was that of a hyena.

Both of our jaws dropped at the thought of a pack of hyenas living on an abandoned plantation in North Carolina. I had heard stories in the past about American hyenas, but the majority of those stories was rooted in cryptozoology, and never had any real proof to back them up.

Of course, if it was hyenas we were dealing with, that would have certainly explained the laughing we heard prior to being chased out of the woods. But this all was entirely unlikely.

People think I am crazy enough as it is, chasing ghosts and monsters, and the last thing I needed to do was parade around claiming we were stalked by a pack of hyenas in North Carolina.

I could not deny that the photograph Allen had on his phone matched the skull we had lying in the grass. I needed more validation than that. I snapped a few pictures of the skull myself, and from my cell phone emailed an anthropologist and research collaborator.

I wanted to seek an outside professional opinion on what we possibly could be dealing with here.

Allen and I found our way back to the team and I instructed everybody to turn in for the night. The following day was going to be long and exhausting.

As the team started moving to their tents, I stopped for a moment and looked over at the plantation house, wondering what in the hell were we going to find in that house?

Seven in the morning came a little too soon for me. I had barely slept from being so sore and even trying to sleep in one-hundred-degree weather was ridiculous. I was the first person to emerge from a tent that morning and the only thing on my mind was getting back out to the edge of the fields.

I wanted to see if I could find any tracks, hair, or better yet, something dead to examine further. I just had to know what it was we had dealt with mainly because I wanted to be better prepared if that situation arose today.

It wasn't long before Allen emerged from his tent with that same intent look of curiosity I was wearing that morning.

We wasted no time gearing up with a few firearms and cameras. Our mission that morning was to return to the area where we experienced the stalking creatures in hopes of finding answers to our questions.

Allen and I started our long walk across the old field. We reached the area from the night before and immediately started scanning the ground for the remains of an animal.

Thirty minutes of searching turned up nothing, and when I say nothing I mean nothing. It was like we were never there and the events of the previous night never took place.

Allen pointed out that not one shell casing from all of the ammunition we fired was anywhere to be found. So we started scouring the ground once more looking for shell casings. Shotgun shells are quite large and very easy to spot on the ground, yet we found nothing.

The entire previous night appeared as if it had never happened, but we both stood there with dumbfounded looks, certain it had.

We began discussing possible theories as to how and why our ammunition had vanished.

Our minds were racing with ideas. We were desperate to find a closer to this conundrum. Allen suggested that somebody or something must have cleaned up our mess to erase any and all evidence of what took place.

But who would do that, and why? Conspiracy theories started to fly.

This was a very unique case, and maybe there were other people involved trying to keep the truth hidden.

At that point we just laughed at such a notion.

Since we were so close to the edge of the woods we decided to travel forth in search of the remaining slave quarters.

After a few hours, we found what appeared to be the foundation of an old building. This was most likely the missing slave quarters. But its current state rendered it useless to us.

We returned to base camp to report to the others our discoveries. Or, depending on how you look at it, our lack of discoveries.

Allen explained to the crew that all of our ammunition was gone and not a single body of an animal was located. Furthermore, no animal tracks and no tracks of our own were evident. Even the ATV tire tracks did not exist.

This newly found information placed every member of the crew and their brains on overload.

I decided that until we were able to figure out what exactly was happening in the woods, it would be best for us to shift our focus to the plantation house.

We spent the rest of the day preparing our gear and discussing the upcoming evening investigation into the old house.

Later that evening, I received a response from my anthropologist friend concerning the skeleton we had found. She said that without question it was definitely some form of canine. However she was having trouble narrowing it down to an exact breed.

She did agree that the similarities between our discovery and a hyena were disturbing, interesting, and haunting.

This did not ease my mind. There I stood closing in on night two of the investigation and we still knew nothing of the creatures that chased us out of the woods.

When you can't find an answer, you call it paranormal.

I'm certainly not saying that we experienced hounds from hell or devil dogs, although those entities did come up in conversation among the team. But something was out there and it was desperate to remove us from the forest by any means necessary.

I knew what we experienced was real. The self-illuminating eyes, the five figures in the field, and the smoking guns were all documented.

Believe me—I am right there with you thinking this all sounds totally absurd. If I had not witnessed it with my own two eyes, I would have never believed it.

What concerned me now was what we would find in the house itself.

As nightfall approached, the team and I prepared dinner on an open fire to fuel ourselves for the long night ahead.

We were eating and chatting, when Noelle noticed something bizarre. She quickly gathered our attention and pointed out that strange lights were coming from inside the house.

We all sat there staring at the house. Through the window, you could see what appeared to be people walking around with flashlights, from room to room.

We were the only people on the property, so it was very easy to rule out actual human beings with flashlights as what we saw emitting from the windows.

This of course intrigued us all and sparked even more excitement about the upcoming investigation.

Then, without warning, both Noelle and Allen saw a bright white light about the size of a basketball fly from one of the campers and into the fenced yard of the plantation house.

Allen and I quickly jumped the fence and ran full force into the yard in an attempt to find the light. As we stood in the grass, we noticed a similar light coming from the middle of the fields.

We wasted no time jumping the fence once more and running straight toward the glowing sphere. But it seemed no matter how hard we ran we never grew closer to the light.

Eventually, the light was gone. We arrived at the middle of the field where we believed the light to have vanished.

I stopped Allen and quickly asked him to listen. I could hear what sounded like a heartbeat coming from the emptiness in front of us. Allen heard it too.

What exactly did we chase into the field? Did we witness an authentic spirit orb?

Now elements of this case were adding up and really pointing toward the supernatural instead of a living, breathing creature.

After returning to camp, I could tell everybody was itching to get into the house. At the same time, I could see hesitation in all of their eyes.

The air was thick and we all admitted to suddenly feeling emotionally different. There was this unexplainable depression taking all of us over.

I have heard of this in the past. Strong spiritual energy can take a toll on a human's body, according to certain beliefs. This had me wondering how strong exactly this spirit, or spirits, was in order to affect us all the way it did.

It was almost as if the house was calling to us at that point. I was greatly concerned that if we were in fact dealing with some form of evil entity, that going into that house could be a foolish move.

At least in the woods and in the fields we had room to move. In that house we would be confined and if something was going to harm us, it would do it there.

With the latest excitement winding down and everybody collecting themselves, it was time to move on.

It was time to see exactly what was waiting for us in that house.

THREE

The Dog House

It was ten in the evening, with the others and me just moments from walking into a living nightmare inside the old farmhouse. The previous night delivered much excitement as we exited the woods fully unloading our guns into cunning anomalies ... or so we thought.

We were all a bit relieved to be entering the next stage of the case and investigation, which would take us inside the house. Not a single person believed we would be walking into a place much darker and more dangerous than the fields and the forest.

Never before have I experienced such malevolent activity and, to be frank, I hope I never have to again. Absolutely nothing good can come from it. In fact, it will drive a person mad.

Cases such as these are extremely rare, despite what film and television would have you believe. However, none of us were going to turn this down. You can call it morbid curiosity or an undying thirst for the unknown, if you wish.

From the outside, the three-story historic house beckoned your attention. There was a strange and unavoidable magnetism to the place. The building was extremely rundown, inside and out, from lack of care and years of weathering. There were twelve rooms in the house. Thirteen if you count the wide-open attic.

A few pieces of old furniture remained. A couple of battered couches, a few tables, and a few chairs were all to be found. An old spinet piano with yellowing chipped keys and a haunting, flat tone was also in one of the rooms.

The walls were decaying in most rooms, and many sections of the ceiling were borderline collapsing. A few rustic chandeliers dangled for life by a thread of wire, while most of the doors swung freely as if the house itself was breathing. The place had definitely gone to the dogs.

Allen, Noelle, and I entered the home prior to the official investigation to begin set up of surveillance equipment throughout the building.

On the second floor, we discovered bizarre looking footprints in the dust. To be honest, they looked like they came from a gigantic chicken. At the time, we dismissed the footprints as just a unique anomaly, probably coming from insects crawling through the dust.

We placed a thermal imaging camera in the attic, since that's where the claw marks and footprints were found, burned into the ceiling.

While in the house, we were all overcome with uneasiness and reported to each other as such. Even though our colleagues were right outside, we felt miles away, as if trapped in another world. In many ways we were.

Inside the house, I found myself lost in a time long forgotten. However, at the same time I did not feel alone. No matter where you went in the building, an overwhelming feeling of being watched by a thousand eyes quickly took over. It was more than disturbing, to say the least, when we found an old knife stuck in one of the walls. What happened here?

As Allen and I continued placing the surveillance, Noelle decided to scout out the remainder of the house. She was drawn to the room with the old piano.

After setting up the thermal imaging camera in the attic, Allen and I proceeded downward, to the second level. The stairs to the attic were old, worn, wooden planks that creaked and cracked with every step. The stairs were steep, so to be sure, taking your time was a must.

The staircase from the second level to the first level was of a spiral design. This was fairly unique for a house built in the early 1800s. The spiral was not sleek and round and flowing, like modern day designs. This spiral was square.

As Allen and I approached the spiral staircase, we both stopped suddenly, to the sound of a door closing on the first level. We knew Noelle was somewhere in the building.

Allen used his radio and called the other members of the team, to see if one of them had entered the building. We discovered they were all still waiting at base camp for our return. Noelle said she heard the sound too, and had not moved as she was sitting by the piano.

I dismissed the door closing as simply being from the hand of Mother Nature's wind, until something astonishing occurred. Allen was in front of me by a good six feet as we approached the top of the stairs, when out of nowhere he was thrown back against the wall, ultimately collapsing to the ground. My stomach sank as I stood in shock from what I just had witnessed. This was absolutely unbelievable and massively incredible.

I immediately ran to Allen's aid. He was just as disoriented as I was. Allen is a big boy, weighing well over two hundred pounds. It would take quite the force to lift him up and throw him against a wall.

The scary part in all of this was the fact that nothing was there to do it. An invisible force prevented him, in a very quick and violent manner, from moving any farther toward the stairs. It was as if something was telling us in a very dramatic way that we were not leaving. Of course, maybe something was testing us.

Allen stood up and shook off the incident. All he could do was laugh and shake his head and look at me in bewilderment. We decided to proceed once more, this time being a little more on guard.

Down the stairs we went without further incident. At this point, I considered what happened to Allen as a message or a warning. We met up with Noelle in the piano room and she asked us what that big bang sound was. Allen and I both looked at each other, and then told her about what happened.

We returned to base camp and briefed the team on the terrifying experience that just took place. Nobody could believe what they were hearing. Half of the team lit up in excitement, while the other half looked completely scared to death. Now was the time to investigate.

We knew, from all our years of experience in this field, that six of us creeping all at once through a house of this nature was going to make too much noise and contaminate any findings we may think we have.

Even considering what had just happened to Allen, and against my better judgment, we decided to go into the house in pairs, for thirty minutes at a time. If a particular pair did not return or respond to radio contact after thirty minutes, the rest would enter the building as a safety precaution.

The first to enter would be Allen, Valere, and Kai. However, Kai would never make it past the front door. The German Shepherd refused to step over the threshold. He simply turned around and ran back to base camp with the rest of us. Allen and Valere proceeded, regardless.

I watched them both enter the house, with the door closing behind them. I anticipated the worst. Something was telling me that tonight would be one for the books. Valere and Allen decided to begin their investigative work in what we dubbed the piano room. The room was immediately to the right upon entering the building.

Moments after entering the room, their attention was grabbed by a large oval mirror sitting on the piano, where one would typically place sheet music. The mirror had a worn wooden frame and the entire thing, just like everything else in this house, was covered in age-old, thick dust. But this is what caught their eye: In the dust, letters had been drawn out as if to relay a message. The letters read, "U DIE U," and took up nearly the entire mirror.

At first, you look at something like that and immediately put your guard up. The first thing I thought it meant, once this was brought to my attention, was that somebody or something was insinuating we were going to die. The writing was adolescent, for sure, but a first glance translation reads, "YOU DIE, YOU." It didn't take a real genius to figure that one out. That may seem very simple, but sometimes simplicity is all you need to get a point across.

Later research after the fact would turn up nothing on that phrase, or bizarre looking word if you place all the letters together. The best I could find concerning the word "UDIEU" referenced a species of fish from overseas. That led to a corny joke on my behalf. Maybe it was because we were fishing for answers. I know, lame joke.

I tried to stretch it a bit, thinking about a time when this farm was in operation. The majority of the slaves owned by the property owner were not native to this country. Hyenas were not native to this country. And the udieu fish was not native to this country. But, like I said, that's a stretch and an idea best left for an episode of the *X-Files*.

While in the piano room, Valere decided to sit at the old antique spinet, staring directly into the mirror. Now we all have different beliefs, different attributes, and an endless array of research techniques, and Valere was no exception. There is a very good reason I assembled the P.I.T. Crew, and it was because each member had a quality the others did not. As time would tell, that has proven to work.

Valere often experimented with the common supernatural belief, rooted in ancient folklore, that mirrors were a gateway to the mind, and possibly other dimensions. Many cultures believe that mirrors allow one to see the darker side of themself. Other cultures believe mirrors open portals to the other side, as if they had recorded a life we once knew. Valere continued staring into the mirror, with Allen firmly standing behind her, contemplating the letters scribbled into the dust.

Allen moved on to investigating the remainder of the room, as Valere continued in her attempt to find a meaning to the mirror discovery. Allen began to notice that the air in the room was getting thicker. It was becoming harder to breathe. He attempted to address this with Valere, but she did not respond. As he started to make his way back toward her she immediately, without warning, began falling back off of the piano bench. Allen reached her just in time. He caught her right before she hit the floor, softening the impact.

Valere was disoriented and displaying stroke-like symptoms. Since she was a nursing professional, I did not hesitate in believing the comparison later on. Staring up at Allen from the floor, she slowly started to regain consciousness. After a little bit of interrogating on Allen's part, Valere described the mirror as turning completely black. She continued by saying she felt paralyzed. Valere made sure it was known that she did not fall off the piano bench. She claimed she was pushed. Valere said it felt as if somebody had placed their hand directly on her chest, pushing her backward.

Considering what they both experienced, neither one of them was wishing to continue through the rest of the house. They needed a few moments to collect themselves, so they returned to base camp outside to report to us what happened. Neither one of them realized they had been in that one room for nearly thirty minutes. We all assumed they had made their way through the entire house.

The two investigators shared their story. Valere sat in her chair by the fire, with a dazed look on her face. Whatever happened had certainly taken a toll on her physically. She said her body was completely drained of energy. She looked at all of us, and called that house a paranormal Pandora's box. This was not sitting with me very well.

From the moment we entered that house, something unexplainable was going out of its way to remove us from it. The disturbing part of the matter was the fact something potentially supernatural was using aggressive techniques to do so.

I decided at this point that I would be the next to enter the building, while Allen and Valere discussed their findings. I grabbed Spencer as my partner for the next thirty minutes. Like our colleagues before us, we closed the door behind us. Spencer and I wasted no time walking directly to the piano room to see the mysterious words written on the mirror.

I sat at the piano for a few moments and even attempted to play a few melodies on it just to see if that would spark any form of activity. Nothing happened.

We decided to start moving through the rest of the house. As we approached the bottom of the steps, both Spencer and I stopped in our tracks when we heard a male voice come from the floor above us. I could not determine what was being said, but it was vivid enough to make me believe somebody was up there talking. No matter what it was, we were going to proceed upward to investigate.

We were cautious going up the stairs, considering what happened to Allen earlier in the day. We walked through room after room on the second floor, and the house remained quiet. Then the sound of something rolling across the attic floor above us broke the silence.

Spencer and I moved toward the attic door. As I opened the door to the attic steps, a white marble came bouncing down at us. This obviously answered the question of what was rolling around up there. I grabbed the marble to examine it, but it was just your run-of-the-mill, everyday marble.

Spencer seemed a little more reserved at this point. She said she was really starting to feel uneasy. As we continued talking, the sound of someone walking above us ended the conversation. The sound of footsteps was so convincing, I was hard-pressed to believe that an actual living, breathing human being wasn't up there. I mean really, if you think about it, this place had been abandoned for years and it's not too out there to consider that maybe a homeless individual had moved in. Luckily, I was armed just in case, and law enforcement was waiting outside by the fire.

We made our way up the steep staircase to the attic. The attic was a large open room. The staircase was precisely in the middle. There were two windows in front and two windows behind. The attic spanned the entire length of the house. The windows, at this time of night, gave off a menacing presence. They were like the house's eyes, watching your every move.

There was a doorway on both sides of the attic, which led to the rafters. I was curious to see what could possibly be found in there, so I directed Spencer to follow me behind the walls. I noticed immediately the danger lying ahead, behind the walls. There were no floors. The only footing provided was nearly two-hundred-year-old wooden rafter beams that creaked, as if to break with every step. To play it safe, we sat immediately inside the door on one of those not-so-welcoming beams. One wrong step, and the second floor would say hello to you real fast.

I decided to turn off our lights and conduct a communication session with the two of us sitting there. A little a bit of moonlight broke through a few cracks in the roof, but light was at a minimum. I asked direct questions. I asked about age, gender, motive, death, and life. But suddenly, I stopped, mid-sentence, when I noticed something moving at the opposite end of the house. I said, "Holy shit!" with excitement.

Something was moving. Something was down there across this death trap, adjacent to Spencer and me. I asked Spencer if she could see it and she confirmed she could. My eyes were having such a terrible time focusing in the darkness. I kept squinting and opening and closing my eyes, in an attempt to focus better. But all I could make out was what appeared to be a black mass or a shadow, slowly swaying back and forth on that last rafter beam.

The sound of scratching led me to believe it was an animal. Maybe it was a raccoon. That idea was quickly removed from my head when a terrifying guttural growl came from the same direction. I immediately turned on a flashlight and aimed it that direction.

I can't say for sure whether it was my eyes adjusting from complete blackout or the flashlight itself, but for a split second I could have sworn I saw something about three feet tall and solid black crouched there. It looked like it was hunched over, meaning that when it stood it would be double the height. Spencer did not see it. At the moment I turned on my flashlight, she was fumbling for hers. Whatever it was had vanished.

We had spent just a little bit over a half hour in the building, so returning to base camp to file our report was next on the agenda. Spencer and I made our way back down through the house without incident. After returning to meet with the others, I grabbed a laptop to transfer the surveillance video recently documented.

I described to the rest of the team the attic incident, the voices, the marble, and the footsteps. I immediately started reviewing the rafter section, after transferring the footage to the laptop. The entire team stared at the laptop screen, hoping to catch a glimpse of what I saw when turning on the flashlight. Unfortunately, when the light came on, the camera needed to refocus for a few seconds to adjust to the new lighting. This resulted in completely failing to document the unknown entity.

Allen reminded me that the thermal imaging camera had been documenting the entire time so if something was, in fact, in there with us, that camera would certainly have caught it on film. The team sat in silence around the fire. I think they were all awaiting my next move.

I started asking each of the investigators their impressions thus far. Many of them were leaning toward the demonic; it was unanimous that something with evil intent, demon or not, resided inside that house.

As we all sat there discussing, I noticed that Allen was staring off into the fire. He wasn't moving. I addressed him, but got no response. Everybody stopped talking and I attempted to address him again. He still refused to move or speak. I stood up and yelled his name, simply thinking he was playing a joke. But it was no joke when his entire body started falling forward and out of his chair, straight toward the campfire.

I leaped to catch him and it took all of my might to hold his body back from the fire. He was completely stiff. The rest of the team jumped to help me pull him backward. Allen fell back away from the fire, still in his chair.

He then went into a full body seizure. We all struggled to hold him but his strength was too much for us. During his seizure he completely destroyed the plastic chair he was sitting in. After about three minutes the seizure stopped.

I was leaning over Allen, saying his name again and again, in hopes of getting a response. I asked him if he knew who I was and he slowly responded with a slur, and said my name. He then looked at me and said, "Give me a cigarette." We all kind of chuckled at that, but the seizure completely drained Allen.

We gave him his cigarette and he smoked it while lying in the grass on his back staring up at the rest of us. He said the last thing he remembered was talking about the thermal camera, then he lost all touch with reality. A few others and I picked him up off the ground and escorted him to one of the campers and into a bed. Within seconds, Allen was asleep and snoring away.

The crew collected themselves once again around the campfire. I said I was going back into that house and straight to the attic, in an attempt to document the black mass.

I asked Noelle to join me. She was the newest addition to the team and looking back, she really was thrown to the wolves with this being her first active case. She was also very deductive and an artist. So at least if she saw what I did, she could sketch it out and we would have something to go by. Into the house she and I went, directly to the attic.

Only a few moments had passed once we reached the attic, when another white marble started rolling across the floor. Now as old as this house is, every move you make results in creaking and cracking, and I was starting to believe that maybe we were causing things to move, simply by moving ourselves. I just could not fathom what a white marble would have to do with anything, otherwise.

I started another communication session at the top of the staircase. Both Noelle and I asked direct questions. One question in particular yielded a very questionable response. Noelle had asked if the spirit there was male. Both she and I immediately heard a male voice say, "Yes." Only this male voice was hauntingly familiar. He sounded just like Allen.

We looked at each other and asked simultaneously if the other had heard the voice. I said I did but asked her what she heard exactly. She confirmed the word "yes," which was exactly what I heard. She also said it sounded like Allen, and I too confirmed that. But Allen was asleep in one of the campers, recuperating from an intense seizure that almost burned him alive.

Now, one had to consider the intelligence of what we were dealing with. Could this entity be mimicking us, as another technique to intimidate or lure us into another intense situation? I instructed Noelle to follow me behind the walls of the attic, so I could show her exactly where Spencer and I sat, and where this entity was seen.

We both knew we had to get to the other side of those rafters to fully investigate. So carefully and very slowly we proceeded to take baby steps across the hazards of the ceiling. Noelle cringed with every step. We held hands to keep each other close, just in case one would fall.

I felt like Indiana Jones waiting for some booby trap to send us falling. Only my Holy Grail at the end of the tunnel wasn't a cup. We made it. We stood at the back of the rafters underneath the old roof, looking back at the distance we traveled. I will admit I thought, "Shit, I have to go back across all of this again."

I scoured the area where I originally saw the black mass, only nothing was there. Noelle leaned against the outer wall of the attic, as I stood about three feet in front of her. I kept my footing spread across two rafters to keep my weight evenly distributed.

I told Noelle that Spencer and I were in a complete blackout when this thing came out. So we turned our lights off. Only a few moments had passed, when that same intimidating, guttural growl made an audible appearance again. The area around us grew extremely cold. Any other time during the summer, when one is directly under a roof, sweating is standard. But this was completely unorthodox.

There was enough moonlight shining through, so Noelle and I could see each other. I looked at Noelle and her face said a thousand words. I think the appropriate way to describe her look was that of seeing a ghost. That was the one time the infamous phrase actually felt true to its meaning. Her face was frozen and pale white. Noelle's eyes were as round as saucers. She wasn't staring at me. She was staring past me.

Without a word spoken, she reached out and grabbed my vest tightly. She pulled me across the beams and into her chest. I asked her if she was all right, and what in the world she was doing. She gripped me hard with her eyes tightly shut. I kept saying her name until she responded. Noelle finally broke out of her trance and demanded we get out of that area. I could tell she was shaken up about something but she would not explain that to me right away.

We made our way back across those lovely, uninviting beams and back into the attic. It was then she would tell me what she saw.

Noelle said as we were standing there shortly after the growl, something a little taller than I am appeared behind me. She did not want me to turn around. This really scared her. Noelle said all she could see were these large, self-illuminating red eyes peering from behind my head. That was why she adamantly pulled me away. She knew if something had been said at the time, I certainly would have turned around. But I got what I wanted out of that. Noelle saw it too. Unfortunately, all she saw were the eyes but that was still an important piece to the puzzle, considering the events at Eidolon Fields. It seemed that with every new investigative session in the house, the supernatural quality of the building went up a notch.

Back at base camp, the story was told. Allen was still fast asleep in the camper. Noelle realized that earlier in the day she had left her water bottle in the piano room. She said she was going back in to retrieve it. At first I was a bit hesitant, but then I told her to go ahead. It should only take a moment. But her decision to walk back into that house would ultimately set the stage for the amazing events to come.

As she left, I stared toward the house and watched her enter. I kept my eyes on the house as the rest of us discussed the investigation. Once again, the notion of a demonic haunting was being tossed around. I personally did not need to believe it was a demon. All I needed to believe was what I knew, and that was something in there was pissed off at our presence. We were disturbing the flow and the paranormal Pandora's box, as Valere called it, was fully opened.

While in the house, Noelle went straight to the piano room and grabbed her water bottle. As she passed the staircase to exit the building, a voice from the second floor said a name. Noelle stopped and looked up the stairs. The name that was spoken was very familiar to all of us. The name that was spoken was mine.

Noelle exited the building and ran back to us. She stopped at the campfire with a confused look on her face. Of course I was biting at the bit. Obviously something happened in the three minutes she was in the building. She asked if any one of us came into the house behind her. We all gave a resounding "No."

Then she looked at me and said somebody called out a name from upstairs, and it sounded just like Jeff. Jeff immediately corrected Noelle by saying he had been outside with us the entire time. And he had. I told Noelle she was the only one in the building.

So we found ourselves again with yet another experience to ponder, which led to this thing using our own voices for manipulation. Of course the big question at this time was more about what was said. Noelle looked at me and said the voice said, "Stephen."

I jumped up from my chair without hesitation, and informed the rest of the group that I was going into the house alone. For whatever reason, the ghost or monster or demon or whatever it was, wanted me in that building and it wanted me in it alone.

The rest of the team advised against it, but I assured them I would stay in constant radio contact. I instructed the whole team to enter the building if they did not hear from me every five minutes.

After swiftly grabbing my camera and entering the forsaken house, I immediately walked to the bottom of the stairs.

I glanced up the stairwell and asked aloud if somebody was looking for me. The house remained still.

Standing there thinking this could be the break we were looking for, the sound of a door slamming shut disturbed the silence. That door was the attic door. It had a very distinct sound, which was much different than any other in the house. There was my invitation. Whatever was asking for me wanted me to come upstairs. I had no choice really. Although admittedly, I was a tad bit scared at the whole situation.

Slowly, one step up was taken at a time. As I approached the top of the steps a bitter coldness surrounded me. I was just about to reach the second floor. My foot was in mid step. Then it happened. One of the most remarkable paranormal experiences I have ever had was about to be set in motion.

The only thing more terrifying than what was about to take place was the violent event I fell victim to as a ten-year-old boy nearly twenty-four years earlier. I wrote about that experience in my first book, *Paranormal Investigator: True Casefiles of a Paranormal Investigator.* Here I was, just a moment away from feeling something I hadn't felt in over two decades.

As my foot was about to touch down onto the second-floor landing, I was struck extremely hard in the face, by an invisible assailant. This force hit me so hard I went straight back and down the steps, ending with a hard slam to the wall and falling to the ground.

The impact of what hit me brought the most extraordinary and unique sensation with it. I describe it as the resistance you feel when placing two magnets together with opposing polar ends. I could feel the magnetism and the energy striking me.

I barely had a moment to comprehend what had happened when a very threatening guttural growl came from just a few feet in front of me. The sound was so animalistic. It sounded like a large dog in the middle of a standoff with a predator.

I sat there on the floor in a panic. I immediately grabbed my radio and contacted the team at base camp. I wanted Allen and I wanted him in there now. Fortunately for me, Allen had recently surfaced from the camper and was back with the team. He wasted no time responding to my call.

Allen came running into hell without a question asked. He looked at me with authentic concern on his face. He asked me what the hell had happened and why my face was bleeding.

I did not realize my face was bleeding so I turned my camera around to record myself. I flipped the monitoring screen of the camera so I could see. I was speechless. There were three slashes down my face and across my cheek.

Now those of us well versed in the paranormal world know that three scratches or cuts typically relate to demonic, or even satanic, mythology. That was all I needed ... more demon talk from the crew.

I quickly briefed him on the attack. I told him the thing was upstairs and if we wanted to know more, now was the time. Allen and I very hesitantly made our way toward the second floor. We arrived without incident and entered the first room to our left.

Standing just inside the doorway, the sound of scratching could be heard from the adjacent room. My camera was aimed through the doorway across from us. Through that door was a room with a table sitting in the center of it.

I did not realize it at the time but the camera was capturing something very vital to this case. I was too busy whispering to Allen about the cuts on my face and the attack to realize what was being filmed right in front of us. I was really shaken up by all of this and could barely catch my breath.

We made our way to the bottom of the attic stairs and sure enough that door was closed. Into the attic we went, without incident. Down from the attic we came, without a problem. It wasn't until we started making our way back to the first floor when our exploring would take another turn for the worse.

I was leading the way downward when Allen was struck in the back and shoved from behind. He was forced into my back, resulting in us both tumbling down the steps. Needless to say, I was growing a bit tired of that. At this point, I felt like I was walking away from a car accident.

The two of us were flat out on the floor below staring up through the stairwell and into the heart of hell. We both made sure the other was all right physically and we were, considering. On the other hand, our mental state was wrecked.

I started laughing like a mad man. Then Allen started laughing like a lunatic. This laughter was originating from multiple sources. For one, I seem to do that a lot after surviving something extremely dangerous. This happens a bit too much.

Secondly, I think we were both laughing at the excitement of the house and the unbelievable factors in play. For us, this was what we lived for. We lived for the real deal, because we were the real deal.

Our laughter ended when the rest of the team started calling us on the radio to check in. Allen and I walked out of the building and straight to the team.

I wish I could sugarcoat what was said but the first words out of Valere's mouth were, "What the hell happened to you two?" Valere and Spencer ran up to me immediately noticing the blood and cuts across my face. Noelle wasted no time taking pictures of the bodily damage. Allen and I both had bruises all over our bodies.

The nurse side of Valere came out and she started examining the wounds on my face. I just crashed at that point. I started sobbing and felt like I had no energy left in my body. The entire team was drained and emotional.

Rick stepped up and suggested that the entity inside the house was trying to take down all of the men. He believed that if we were stopped, the whole team would be stopped.

He said it attacked me since I was the head of the crew, and it attacked Allen because he was my right-hand man. This was an interesting enough thought to ponder and did make sense. However, at this point, I could no longer with a clear conscious place any of us in the line of fire again.

Maybe this entity beat me. Maybe it beat us. Maybe there was more than one. The facts certainly favored that idea. But I saw all I needed to see.

Once again we all gathered around the campfire. The investigation was over. I called it. It was done. I didn't hear an argument from anybody. The P.I.T. Crew wanted to see the video from the point I entered alone, to the point Allen and I exited the house together. I obliged.

The laptop received the video transfer, and we all sat around that seventeen-inch screen like a bunch of kids waiting for Christmas morning. The sound of gasps, curse words, cheers and jeers from the crew surrounded the laptop with every minute of video seen.

However, two more twists in this narrative were about to make all of the risks taken worthwhile. The blood, sweat, and tears were about to be rewarded.

The video was reaching the point just after Allen came to my aid. This was when Allen was trying to calm me down, and my camera was shooting through the doorway aimed at a table in the other room.

I instantly stopped the video after making a remarkable discovery. Underneath the table was something I had never seen before in my life. I can't believe this thing was only a few feet away from me and Allen at the time. But my camera caught a creature sitting in the dark shadow of the table.

I went back to the point I saw this thing in the video to see if the rest of the crew would notice it and they did. We must have gone back and watched that little creature three dozen times.

I froze a part of the video to a single frame and what we were looking at came straight out of your darkest nightmares. This was a creature with supernatural qualities. The head was like that of the classic gargoyle. There appeared to be two horns protruding from it.

Since it was in the shadows, the entire body was not visible. We could only see from the shoulders forward, but it was easy to believe this creature standing on its hind legs would be just a little taller than me.

In the video, the mouth of this menacing-looking dog seemed to be opening and closing as if it was trying to say something. One of the crew suggested that it was mimicking what Allen and I were discussing at the time the video was taken.

The one foot we could see in the video had two long claws in the front, with one long claw at the heel of the foot. Inch-long nails were attached to each. Three nails equal three scratches. I think we found our giant chicken.

Now I had to try to wrap my head around a supernatural being that not only could cloak itself and manifest into different forms, but could also speak and make physical contact with us. That was a hard thing to swallow, and still is to this day.

We all felt accomplished at that point. A discovery of this nature is huge in our line of work. But the final twist would have to wait until morning.

Shortly after the excitement died down over the amazing discovery, we turned in for the night. No one was going back into that house until the sun came up and when it did, we would all go back in together to retrieve our equipment. Into my tent I went at four-thirty in the morning.

The sun arrived a little too soon for all of us. I emerged from my tent, lit a cigarette, and stared at the house. My eyes were squinting and burning from the sun. I guess that's a downfall of being a creature of the night.

One by one, members of the P.I.T. Crew welcomed the day with bellyaching and groans. After a quick breakfast, we entered the house to break down the surveillance equipment and remove all other research tools.

The entire team was off. Everybody seemed depressed and it went without question that we were very short with one another. The team was exhausted and so was I. The house, the woods, and the fields pushed us to the limit. We would be leaving the house, but the house would never be leaving us. You just can't forget about such a remarkable yet horrific experience.

After all of the equipment was loaded back up into the trailers and all of our things were packed away, I pulled out the thermal imaging camera that had been monitoring the attic. I really didn't have time to review it all since we would be departing soon, but I at least wanted to look at the section documenting when Spencer and I were in the attic and I saw the black mass.

I sat in a chair facing the fields with the thermal camera in my lap. It wasn't long before I located the section I wanted to review. I screamed, "Holy crap!" That, of course, brought the attention of the others.

We did it. We captured it. That camera caught a full-bodied apparition and it was right in the room with Spencer and me. On the video you could see us enter behind the walls of the attic. You could hear my communication session. You could also hear my, "Holy shit" when I believed to be seeing something in front of us. This video proved I did.

On the thermal camera a large, blue sphere about the size of a basketball appeared from the right of the screen. It slowly moved across the attic, growing larger. This was happening during my communication session. By the time it reached the doorway to enter behind the wall, its shape had changed into a full-bodied entity.

It looked like a six-foot man standing there. He seemed to be peering into the doorway where Spencer and I were sitting. The figure moved through the wall and it was at that moment I stopped my communication session and said, "Holy shit."

The timing could not have been any better. The entity appears as some sort of energy ball and then becomes a man walking into my direct line of site. That was when I saw the black mass. It was perfect. The team and I had found our Holy Grail.

This is honestly the best piece of physical evidence I have in my possession that promotes the belief of life beyond our own physical existence. Needless to say despite our tired souls, we were all grinning ear to ear. I turned off the camera and packed it away and we all started our long journey back home.

To this day I guard that footage. We walked away with some of the most captivating pieces of evidence in favor of the supernatural.

This whole situation was completely insane. But this was a case that people deserved to hear. I can sit here and tell you, straight from a person who has spent a great deal of his life researching the unknown, that this is true. Coming across such a dark force is extremely rare. But it does happen. I'm just happy we lived so the story could be told.

However, the emotional toll this case took on us would ultimately play a role in the demise and decommissioning of the P.I.T. Crew. But I still wonder to this day what is going on at that property, and will I ever see it again? The current owner has prevented any further research from being conducted, from fear that he too may fall victim to whatever evil is dominating that property.

Following our discoveries, in fear of his own well-being, Mr. Scotts ceased renovation of the property and once again the woods, the fields, and the house are empty ... or are they? We joke among each other about people who question the paranormal or flat out dismiss it altogether.

I usually say, "Throw them in the dog house, and then ask the question again if they make it out."

FOUR

The Piper Room

Shortly after the incident at Eidolon Fields, I separated from my wife. Working in the field of paranormal research consumed my life. My obsession with the afterlife took a harsh toll on my personal well-being. I moved in with Allen and Spencer, who were two of my investigators. They had a modern, three-bedroom apartment on the fourth floor, and luckily for me one of those bedrooms was vacant.

I had ordered the P.I.T. Crew to take a few months off in hopes all of them, including myself, could mentally break away from the haunting effects of the Eidolon and Dog House case. We all left that case as different people. We treated each other differently. All of our personalities seemed to have had a newly found negative quality attached to it. It was time for a break. Some of the investigators welcomed the break, while others refused and kept on working anyway. Tension was high. We were no longer operating as a team. Independent research was being sought out.

About six months later, the remaining members of the team started taking cases again. I accepted one in Aiken, South Carolina. At the time, I was thinking a case involving a hotel would be fairly uneventful and a nice change of pace, considering the events from months ago. I was wrong. Just when I thought I had witnessed it all in the field of paranormal research, I blacked out, went into a seizure, and documented some bizarre phenomena.

Up until now, this was an undisclosed case I had chosen to keep locked up tight and out of the public eye. When I decided to release the files of my most bizarre and extreme cases, this one was left questionable, simply due to the fact that nothing like this had ever happened to me before. I really did not wish for my sanity to be questioned.

Frankly, I never believed something like this could actually happen. But it did, and a few shots of vodka later found me transcribing and transferring the events documented in the official case file to this book.

Sunday, February 19, 2012, is a day I will never forget, yet I will never remember. When I loaded my truck and headed north the Friday prior, I would have never believed I was traveling toward becoming a temporary monster.

This case reminds me of the classic wolfman story and those tales of the man who shape-shifts into a cold-blooded, animalistic killer. That monster we all know with undeniable characteristics, howling at the moon and carrying out disturbing and violent actions fueled by the need to feed and to taste blood. And when returning to human state, our man never has any recollection of the events that had taken place.

Although this case had nothing to do with anything rooted in cryptozoology or fictitious monsters created by movie studios, this case did share one similarity to the infamous werewolf. Like the man-turned-beast-turned-man, I suffered a loss in time and memory, and became an entirely different person with very few of my own thoughts to go on. Part of me believes that an intelligent force yet to be understood knew I was coming. Part of me believes it wanted to finish what it had started nearly four years ago.

In 2009, I answered a call to investigate a case in southwestern South Carolina that involved a room in a commercial building no person could bear to occupy. My findings revealed an extremely strong and dangerous electromagnetic field that, under any circumstance, could drive a person mad. In some instances, it did. A few unfortunate individuals ultimately fell to their death from alleged suicide, after being in this room for just a brief moment. In the end, the file was left open, and the case dubbed the "Piper Room" slowly became lost under a stack of demanding research obligations.

However, the question then is the same question now: what on earth could cause such a strong electromagnetic field, intense enough to move objects and cause human beings to completely disregard rational thought and better judgment?

What on earth could create a field powerful enough to cause a person to feel like a metal vice is slowly crushing their skull? The bigger question and possibly the more viable one is what natural or supernatural occurrence can manifest something that incredible, and a man-made object is not the source?

On Friday, February 17, 2012, I left Myrtle Beach, South Carolina, and traveled north to Warsaw, North Carolina, to pick up Noelle, the investigator accompanying me to conduct continued research on the 2009 case. Our arrival at the Piper Room location was not expected until the following day, so management set up lodging for us at a hotel in Warsaw. Little did either of us know that night would act as a prelude to the coming events.

At the hotel, the two of us discussed the upcoming case, until Noelle fell asleep on one of the beds around one in the morning. I remained wide-awake, and occupied my time listening to music on a laptop.

About an hour later I was interrupted and shocked by Noelle having a panic attack on the bed. She was breathing rapidly as her chest was bouncing up and down, in a fashion that reminded me of when paramedics fire off a defibrillator on a person.

This caught me completely off guard, because at no time did she ever tell me of suffering from such a thing. I yelled her name about half a dozen times before she woke up abruptly, gasping for air. From across the room I was screaming at her, asking if she was all right, in hopes of getting a response.

Possession. What the hell is it really? Puppeteering, perhaps? Could the effects of possession be similar to the technical workings of a remote control? A human being involuntarily speaking or moving forcefully by an unseen operator—which ultimately leads to perceived innocence of severe and sometimes brutal actions—defines what the majority would consider being possessed.

Considering that, many people frequently lay religious overtones alongside extreme supernatural cases, involving one or more individuals losing conscious control of their own mind and body. I couldn't help but think that all of us brought a piece back from that old farm house, and it certainly wasn't peaceful.

Noelle composed herself following the panic attack. She was just as surprised as I was and had no real explanation as to what brought it on. Our atmosphere at that time was completely relaxed. We weren't even in the place of investigation, so what in the world, in a normal hotel room, would cause such tension?

Shortly after Noelle calmed down, both of us literally jumped a foot into the air from the sound of a gunshot. The sound echoed through our room. Both of us reacted accordingly, in shock, disbelief, and fear. The sound was so vivid.

I was standing by the desk and Noelle was sitting up on the bed when it happened. At first we just remained still, expecting to hear some sort of commotion outside to follow. I slowly crept to the window to where I could see down into the parking lot. Everything looked normal. No chaos, no screaming, no running.

We put an ear to the wall of the neighboring room, expecting to possibly hear something there. But all we could hear was the couple next door watching television. I was baffled and concerned, and awaiting police sirens. But those sirens never happened. Noelle and I were confused. How could nobody else in the building have heard the gunshot?

The remainder of the night went without incident. Come morning, the purpose of the phantom gunshot was still a mystery. However, a future case would potentially reveal its supernatural origin. We loaded up the vehicle and headed on the four-hour drive to the hotel, where the Piper Room awaited.

We arrived around one in the afternoon, and the staff was courteous and happy to see me again. They made arrangements to allow us to check in early, which was very hospitable. After unloading all of our gear into our room on the third floor, I decided to show Noelle the infamous room, formerly known as 225.

Over the years, the hotel received dozens of complaints from guests about the room. Stories from the staff informed me that most guests would request a new room within an hour of checking in. Some guests, however, would check out in an unfortunate way.

A few people were driven mad in the room, and ultimately jumped to their death from the window. A few others died in the room of heart attacks. Now, the hotel had converted the room into storage for housekeeping. No person is permitted to stay in the room anymore. They even removed the room number from the door.

After showing Noelle the door to the room, we decided to order some food from the in-house restaurant, before tackling the investigation. I knew if either one of us went into that room, all else would be forgotten and we would start investigating. So I wanted to wait until we at least had some food in us.

After about an hour of relaxing in the restaurant, we returned to our room to start prepping the cameras and other equipment. We waited until most guests staying at the hotel had retired for the evening. I wanted the property, and especially the area around Room 225, as quiet as possible.

For this investigation the technique was going to be simple. Noelle and I would enter the room one at a time in fifteen-minute intervals. This would prevent any long exposure to the high electromagnetic fields.

In a normal setting, electromagnetic fields rarely hit high numbers on detecting devices. These fields are everywhere, in houses, businesses, and basically anywhere electronic equipment can be found.

A refrigerator rarely emits fields higher than fifty on the Gauss scale of a detector. A light fixture or standard wiring behind the wall might read anywhere from ten to twenty. There are many variations to this and many things to consider. But as a general rule, those are the numbers to be expected. So what of a room that consists of nothing but linen and towels? That is just another part of the allure and mystery to Room 225.

The time was late and we were ready to begin looking into the forgotten room. Noelle stayed in our room, while I went to the second floor for the first investigation session. Immediately upon entering the room, I could feel the strength of the electromagnetic field. Depending how strong, these fields can cause disorientation, hallucinations, nausea, and paranoia if exposed for a long period of time.

I quickly started scanning the room to see where the fields were stronger. Along the way, the reads on my detector were to be expected. Very subtle reads reflecting the wiring behind the walls were found. That was nothing to write home to mom about. However, as expected from my research, years prior, the reads were off the charts. My devices were detecting fields ranging from five hundred on the gauss scales to well over six hundred. To put it bluntly, this was uncanny and insane. It was truly no wonder why no person could stand to be in the room for very long.

After carefully sweeping the area, I discovered that the field made a large sphere approximately six feet in diameter. After only being in the room for a little over five minutes, I was finding it difficult to breathe. I left the room to report the high reads to Noelle and send her in for her opinion. Noelle entered the room a few minutes after discussing what I experienced. She immediately noticed the air was very thick. Noelle said that she too was having difficulty breathing. Like me, she experienced the same thing, and also documented the extremely high fields. Noelle started to feel a little dizzy and decided to exit the area.

She returned to our room to find me pacing the floor and mumbling to myself in an attempt to make sense of such an abnormal and repetitive occurrence. I immediately said I was going back down to the room. This second visit would yield some other confusing results. I returned to 225, and started filming the area and the field reads from my device.

After about fifteen minutes, I started to get very sharp pains in my head. The pain became so unbearable that I actually hunched over and leaned against a wall. A few seconds later, I composed myself and went out the door. I returned to the room where Noelle and I were staying, to find her sitting on the windowsill, with the window open. I quickly ran over to her, confused as to why she was sitting like that. It really worried me that one wrong move could have led to her falling three stories to the ground. I reached out and pulled her back into the room.

She was a little disoriented and had no recollection as to why she was sitting in the window like that. This concerned me and at this point I told her I did not want her going back down to Room 225.

As we were talking, I noticed one of our cameras lying on the center of the bed. I asked Noelle if she had placed it there and she said no. I grabbed it and discovered the camera had been filming.

We played back the footage. There was no video to be found, but there was audio. All I could hear was Noelle opening the window and the sounds of climbing onto the sill. I was shocked to see no video had been documented. The screen was jet black. That camera had never malfunctioned like that before.

We placed one of our field detectors on the center of the bed. As it should be, the read was very low. Somehow that camera was removed from the case and placed on the bed, without being noticed. Then we started asking questions in hopes of breaking open a line of communication.

Up until this point, I really didn't believe anything supernatural to be the cause of the high fields or the effects of it. Noelle started asking questions that revolved around what we knew of the people who died there. It was that line of questioning that caused the meter to burst from low numbers to high numbers rather quickly. This just does not happen unless a field is present, so something unseen moved closer to that device.

All other questions yielded no result. Only when we would talk about the suicides and deaths did the meter react. At this point I was dying to go back down to 225 for more research. Noelle was hesitant and really did not like the idea of me going back down there. It was at this point that I would forget everything.

We were well into the night and closing in on Sunday morning. Everything else I'm about to write was a result of reviewing my camera and listening to Noelle's testimony after the investigation.

I returned to Room 225. My camera footage showed that I went into the room and started documenting the high levels once again. Like before, I hunched over in pain and started talking in an attempt to communicate with a potential spirit.

You see, it is believed that spirits need some form of energy to communicate, manifest, or move objects. The fields inside 225 were more than enough to do that. I left the room and returned to Noelle. This time I was moving a lot faster and pacing back and forth throughout our room. She said I was spewing nonsense and talking aloud, trying to solve the problem with 225.

Noelle said she never saw me more passionate about something. She said it was like I was determined to sell her an idea about that room, although I never said what that idea was. I was talking nonsense about the Pied Piper and how he would hypnotize rats into following him through the streets and to their death. Room 225 was doing just that. It was like a magnet that I could not break away from. It was a Piper Room.

After Noelle talked me down, she said I laid flat on my back on the bed. Shortly after, I stopped talking nonsense.

About an hour had passed, when I either had a panic attack or a seizure, and startled Noelle. I have never been diagnosed with seizures. I never had one before, and I have not had one since. She said I was breathing in and out really fast. I was shaking and would randomly hold my breath. Noelle said this went on for about twenty minutes until I finally calmed down and fell asleep.

The next morning, I woke up completely disoriented. I asked Noelle what happened during the investigation. I could not remember any of it. If it weren't for her and all of the camera documentation, I would have no idea. We were both more than happy to leave that day. I remember driving Noelle back home and still feeling disoriented. Although the further away I got from the hotel, the better I felt.

After dropping Noelle off back in North Carolina, I returned to Myrtle Beach, South Carolina, to review the material. I asked my head investigator and roommate Allen Bess to review the footage.

During my blackouts and when I was talking, he said that the voice on the recordings did not even sound like me. He said it sounded like somebody else talking, although he knew it was me, because of the video proof. Like me, he was just as amazed at the high level of electromagnetic fields found in that room. Allen was also just as impressed with the lack of memories.

Maybe Noelle's short memory loss was a result of not being exposed to the fields for as long as I was. I just could not stop returning to that room. It was like I was being controlled or hypnotized. Needless to say, I'm glad that investigation is over. I may never find the reason why that room has such a magnetic draw to it. Maybe some things are best left alone.

Is it spiritual, or is it simply something that can be explained scientifically? I just don't know. Were we communicating with one of the room's victims? If the room's victims were haunting the property now, what originally caused the room to be what it is to begin with? There are still so many unanswered questions.

But just like Room 225 mesmerized me and drew me to it, something else was still was drawing me and the rest of us. So the haunting memories of past investigations were far from over.

FIVE

New Tenant

We have all heard about the lost puppy following somebody home. But what if a ghost followed you home? Sounds like a dream come true for a person like me, but in this case, the antagonistic guest was, without question, unwelcome.

At this point, I was really beginning to consider that the entity we faced at Eidolon Fields had somehow latched on to not only me, but other members of the team. Something dark was around Noelle and me all weekend. Could it all be related?

I returned to Allen and Spencer's apartment after a weekend researching the Piper Room. I was extremely spiritually charged after what I was subjected to there. Allen and Spencer were out of town for a few days, so I was left to protect the fort, care for their dog, and try not to destroy anything, so to speak.

It was Monday, February 18, 2012. I was exhausted after the weekend and for good reason. I was expecting a fairly uneventful week of reviewing all the documentation from the Piper Room. That did not happen, however.

That evening I was sitting behind my computers, reviewing the video and audio footage captured from the prior weekend's investigation. I was the only one in the apartment and the dog was asleep on the bed. My head was buried in headphones, so it was shocking to hear knocking coming from the living room.

At first I thought Allen and Spencer had returned home much earlier than planned. I took off the headphones so I could listen. I heard a series of knocks again.

I left my bedroom and proceeded to the living room. Everything seemed fine and in place. The knocking had stopped so it was nearly impossible for me to pinpoint where exactly it had originated. Of course, living in an apartment building, just about any anomalous sound is dismissed as coming from other tenants.

As I was standing in the living room, I heard a slight click and then I noticed the door to the laundry room was slowly opening. The click I heard must have been the door unlatching. My guess was the door wasn't fully closed to begin with and a shift in the building or some other subtle vibration was just enough to make it move.

I started walking toward the laundry room door to investigate. I was immediately startled by the sound of a pot falling in the sink. Again I tried to rationalize by simply dismissing it. The pot could have been sitting on the edge of the sink and my walking around made it fall into the sink.

I started down the hallway to return to my bedroom. I immediately noticed that the doors to my bedroom, the storage room, and the bathroom were wide open. I knew for a fact that the storage room door was closed and always had been. The room was being used for storage. We rarely went in there.

Another interesting fact to point out is the lights were on in both the storage room and bathroom. Considering all of these anomalous events, I decided to power up one of my video cameras, grab an electromagnetic field tester, and start documenting the occurrences if anything else was to happen.

As I started recording, a male voice was heard saying, "Hey." At this moment I knew that the activity I had been witnessing was supernatural. I could not explain away the voice. A man spoke and he did so directly beside me. Someone or something wanted my attention and he got it.

Shortly after returning to the living room, I heard the sound of a doorknob shaking. Allen's master bedroom door was slightly vibrating and the doorknob was shaking just enough to be visible and make sound.

I tested the door for high electromagnetic fields. Logging over point eighty in Gauss mode was extremely unique for a modern apartment with nothing electrical running through the door. This told me that nothing man-made was the cause.

With the door still vibrating, I reached out to grab the doorknob and enter the bedroom. Just before my hand gripped the doorknob, the shaking visibly stopped. Without a moment of silence, from the kitchen, I heard one of the cabinet doors close. The entity was playing cat-and-mouse.

I started walking into the kitchen when I caught a brief glimpse of a cabinet door closing. This was downright eerie. No cabinet doors were open prior to this and physically watching one close without human intervention gave me an unsettling feeling in my own home.

The atmosphere and mood in the apartment began to change. I started feeling nervous and paranoid. That rarely happens to me, but there was some sort of energy in the air that felt negative. The feeling was reminiscent of the Piper Room. This worried me severely. Did something come back with me? Did I inadvertently place myself and my roommates in danger?

As I was standing there contemplating the events, a lamp from across the living room fell over and onto the floor, causing me to jump in a panic. The lamp was about six feet tall and could not simply fall over with it being pushed.

When the lamp hit the floor, the light bulb at the top started flickering rapidly for about two seconds. I ran over to the lamp to log any obscure electromagnetic field data. Sure enough, the reads were exceptionally high and way beyond what a lamp of this style was capable of producing.

I set the lamp back to the original upright position. Before I could do anything else, the loudest, most ear piercing squeal consumed the room. The sound was so high in pitch it literally brought me to my knees in pain. I dropped my camera and covered my ears. The sound was coming from the television set, which was not powered on. The painful high tone lasted for about fifteen seconds before stopping abruptly. Days later I would ask Allen and Spencer about the sound and they would confirm it was abnormal and never happened to the television before.

At that moment, I could not help but feel that something was building here. The activity was heightening and very quickly. I stood still in the living room awaiting the next wave of paranormal occurrences.

From down the hall I heard what sounded like a door closing. After quickly running to the hall, I found myself dumbfounded, immediately noticing that all three doors were closed. From underneath the doors, I could see the lights had been turned off as well.

I slowly proceeded to the end of the hall to examine the doors to the bedroom, storage room, and bathroom. I opened the door to my bedroom first and inside nothing appeared to be out of place. Nothing was noticeably wrong inside the other two rooms as well.

What happened next, I have to admit, was a bit intense. After so many years in this field, I am quite desensitized. However, following the events of Eidolon Fields, my perspective has changed somewhat. There are things we cannot explain out there, that can and will hurt you. I can say that with confidence, having been attacked a few times in my life. Moments like these make me consider the possibility that something out there has been following me since I was a child. I have no idea as to why, but it concerns me that all of these events are building toward something unpleasant. In *True Casefiles of a Paranormal Investigator,* I speak in great detail about the attack I endured when I was ten years old. Many cases in recent years have shown similarities in behavior and characteristics.

I snapped out of my thoughts, and while standing at the end of the hall I started to play back the last few minutes of footage from my video camera. Sure enough, I could hear the doors closing when I was standing in the living room.

I continued to review the footage. All of a sudden I could hear a scraping sound coming from the edge of the hall. I immediately started documenting with the camera again.

I stood my ground and kept filming as the scraping started coming down the hall slowly toward me. I best describe it as a person walking with both arms out allowing their fingernails to scrape the wall as they continue down the hall.

This was creepy. Standing there, and blatantly hearing someone or something walking toward me, yet I can't see them, was absolutely terrifying. What do you do? I had no defense if this entity were to become violent. I was standing there accepting the fact that the next few moments could result in something devastating.

As the scraping grew closer and closer to me, the reads on the electromagnetic field detector went higher and higher. I was standing still. That meant that whatever was creating this magnetic field was moving. This was not coming from some stagnant electrical device.

I started asking questions. I wanted to know who or what it was. Then, like a flash in the pan, the scraping stopped. The weight of the air seemed to have lifted at that moment. I sat in the living room for the next few hours hoping something else would happen, but it never did.

I decided to review all of the footage to see if I had missed anything during the experience. Sure enough, I did. During those intense moments when the entity was cornering me in the hall, a few disturbing voices were captured.

Sensitive readers beware. In a low, rough, guttural tone, the first voice said with a little less tact, "Screw you," in a very angry response to me asking, "Who are you?" The second voice captured was simply a low, deep chuckle. Following the chuckle, the scraping stopped. Was this entity playing with me the entire time or was the spirit sending a message?

The next few days were quiet. Nothing else happened that I could not explain away by conventional means. At the end of the week, Allen and Spencer returned to the apartment. I wasted no time sharing my experience with them, and it goes without saying that all of the video footage amazed and shocked them.

As the three of us were sitting in the living room, the dog began to stare off toward the master bedroom door. The dog was growling as if to warn us of a trespasser. But nothing was there that we could see.

It took a while for the dog to calm down. Allen literally had to place him in a cage and in another room to get him to stop growling. The dog seeing something that we could not added to the previous events.

The next night, Allen and Spencer went to work leaving me once again alone in the apartment. With the exception of using the bathroom, I stayed in my room the entire night.

It was just after midnight when I heard somebody enter the apartment. At least that's what it sounded like to me. I had heard people come in and out of the front door numerous times. This sounded just like it. I assumed at the time it was either Allen or Spencer returning from work. I would later find out I was wrong.

I fell asleep and about an hour later I woke up to the sound of my bedroom door opening. Again, believing that Allen and Spencer were home, I just figured it was one of them looking in to see if I was awake.

I remained still on my side, and in the corner of my eye I could tell that someone had walked into the room and was standing at the corner of my bed. A few moments later, the person left, closing the door behind them. I fell back asleep.

A little later I was awoken abruptly by Spencer yelling from the living room, "Oh my god! Stephen!" I leaped out of bed and ran out into the living room. My jaw dropped at what I saw.

Spencer was pointing at the furniture with her mouth wide open as well. She just kept repeating, "Stephen, did you do this?" "What the hell happened?"

The living room was completely ransacked. Every piece of furniture was placed upside down. The couches, the chairs, the end tables and the coffee table had all been flipped over precisely in their existing locations and placed on their tops. At first glance, I thought we had been robbed. But nothing was missing.

I could tell Spencer was really shaken up, after I explained to her I had been in my room the entire evening. I questioned her, because I believed that someone entered the apartment just an hour or so ago. Spencer assured me that Allen was still at work and she just left her job to come home.

At this point I was in shock. I said out loud, "Who the hell came in my room then? I thought it was you!" Spencer was surprised to hear this from me. I was convinced a person had opened my door, entered, stood for a moment, and left after closing the door. We quickly called Allen and he immediately left work. We left everything how it was discovered by Spencer.

This all sounds crazy. Believe me I know. If I had not witnessed this myself, I would be extremely skeptical. But it is what it is. Something or someone, without making a sound, strategically placed all the furniture upside down.

One person could not have done this. The couches were too large and heavy. It would have at least taken two people to pull off something like this if it were a prank. We were all relieved it wasn't a break-in, but at the same time, I remained a little nerved up about the situation. I was the only one home and heard nothing from the living room, other than what I thought was one of my roommates returning from work.

Allen arrived at the apartment about forty-five minutes later. His reaction was predictable. He too was extremely surprised, and instantly thought a robbery had taken place. This prompted Allen and me to pull out my surveillance system and wire cameras throughout the entire apartment. We ran cameras to each area where I had previously documented supernatural activity.

There were too many questions at this moment and not enough answers. Without a doubt, something supernatural had been taking place in the apartment since I returned from the Piper Room. Whatever it was did not appear to be friendly and was attempting to intimidate us without resorting to actual harm.

Over the next week, Allen and I spent many hours reviewing the surveillance footage from times when none of us were present in the apartment. Unfortunately, nothing turned up. It would seem that this entity was very aware of what we were doing and was not giving up the least little bit for us to document. Why?

The entity was no stranger to me and went out of his way to get my attention, even knowing that filming was taking place. He wasted no time turning the living room upside down to gain attention. So why stop once surveillance cameras were documenting? I wish there would have been some sort of closure to this particular haunting. It involved me and a few of my fellow investigators, with no real motive that we could figure out.

The three of us relocated a few months later. Allen and Spencer remained living together in a new house, while I moved to North Carolina. Fortunately, or unfortunately, depending on how you look at it, I didn't move alone. Something came with me.

SIX

Inside Man

After leaving the apartment, I moved to a house in Ocean Isle, North Carolina. The location was quiet and the home sat nestled beneath a wooded area. The interior was completely furnished with extremely dated furniture and décor. It was quite obvious the original owner was elderly before vacating the property and turning it into a rental. The paintings were the stereotypical, scary looking, old portraits of children and adults.

The owner's son, Layne, was handling the rental and any repairs that the property might have needed. Immediately upon touring the home, I had a dozen questions for him. There were strict rules that came along with becoming the new tenant. First and foremost, nothing could be removed from the property. The furniture had to stay and none of the old paintings or assorted décor could be relocated. Everything needed to stay exactly where it was.

I understood the owner not wanting anything removed, but I did not understand why nothing could be moved within the home. Even Layne really couldn't give me a logical explanation as to why. All he could say was that was his mother's wishes. I would later think back on that conversation and wonder if his mother knew something else was in that home, and she did not want to disturb or anger it.

The next thing I had to agree to was to care for the owner's dog, Rus, who was a grey Jack Russell Terrier. That wasn't a problem for me, since I'm an avid dog lover and I certainly didn't mind the company.

During the tour, I noticed that both the front and back doors to the home had security bars installed on the inside. It was evident they were placed as a barricade to keep anything from the outside busting down the door. Of course I had to know, why? That concerned me a little, causing worry that the area might not be safe and break-ins were common.

Layne assured me the security bars were installed by his mother. He explained to me that in the 1980s, a man had broken into the home and raped her. His older brother, who luckily happened to be stopping by for a visit, entered the home and ultimately shot and killed their mother's assailant. He died in the house.

I understood, after hearing the story, why his mother would be a little paranoid at that point and want to feel much safer. That could also be why the home was laced with angels and religious relics.

I can't lie, however. The creepy décor and vintage furniture, coupled with the fact a man was murdered in the home, completely sold the rental to me. Call me demented, but I saw opportunity.

I moved in within a few days, and it didn't take long to get settled. It also didn't take long for strange things to begin happening. I think it's normal when you move into a new place to be a little nervous, until the place actually feels like home. But I was nervous all the time. I felt very uneasy in the house alone. This was abnormal for me. I have firearms. I have plenty of ways to protect myself. I even had a living burglar alarm with Rus. But I still felt off in the place.

I did an electromagnetic field (EMF) sweep of the home just to rule out any extremely high reads as being the cause of my paranoia. High EMF reads have been known to cause paranoia, delusions, and nausea in people. But the house checked out fine in that department.

After a few weeks, something occurred that put up my paranormal investigator antenna full-time. It was a Saturday afternoon, and I was behind the computer writing and enjoying a few beers. Once again I was buried in headphones, but this time I was listening to music while I wrote.

As I was typing, I heard a light metallic sound come from my left. The sound was light to me since I heard it over the music I was listening to. The sound came from the kitchen. I ignored it at first. Shortly after, I noticed Rus standing stiff and poised beside the chair I was sitting in, with his attention on the kitchen. I kept the headphones on, but like Rus, had my attention on the kitchen.

Then out of nowhere, I heard what sounded like metallic objects being thrown across the room. I did not see anything, but I certainly heard it. This time the sound was much louder, suggesting more force was behind it.

I quickly threw the headphones off and jumped out of my chair. At this point, Rus was growling in the direction of the kitchen, but he refused to move.

Jokingly, I tried coaxing Rus to check it out. Any other time, the dog would take off running, whether anything was there or not, at the sound of my voice suggesting it. Not this time. He was not budging.

I walked out to the kitchen and around the table to discover two beer cans on the floor. I was so confused. I knew less than a half hour ago I had placed those directly into the trashcan. What was truly amazing about this was the fact that I had just emptied the trashcan earlier that day so the only things in it were those beer cans.

That meant somebody or something had to push the swinging lid open, reach down inside, and physically lift those cans out and place or throw them on the floor. This certainly explained the metallic sounds I heard just moments prior.

This was not possible. I was the only person in the house and as I suggested earlier, full paranormal radar was up and running at this point.

As I stood still, waiting for something else to happen, a series of knocks came from the bedroom adjacent to the kitchen. This was not the room I was sleeping in. The room acted more as a guest room so nobody was really ever in there.

I ran back to my bedroom, grabbed a video camera, and immediately started recording. I documented what had previously happened as I approached the guest room. I slowly walked through the room asking aloud if anybody was in there in hopes of gaining a response. After discovering nothing, I started to head back to the kitchen.

Before I could reach the kitchen, I was forced to jump back about three feet from the laughter I heard just around the corner. The laughter was from an older male, and reminded me of how a child laughed after pulling off something mischievous. I was really beginning to think that someone, somehow, was able to get into the home.

I continued into the kitchen and was surprised on one hand, and not on the other, to find nothing. Nobody was there and Rus still stood firmly in the living room, staring into the kitchen like a statue. Something had spooked the dog. He had urinated and the carpet underneath him was completely saturated. He was shaking at this point, too. I wasn't sure whether or not he was shaking from what scared him or shaking because he knows he is supposed to relieve himself outside.

Regardless, the dog's behavior only added to what I had experienced and documented that afternoon. Nothing out of the ordinary happened the rest of the day.

Another week passed without incident, and I decided to share the experience with one of my investigators, Noelle. She came to spend the weekend in the house more so as a friendly visit rather than as a paranormal researcher. But after I shared my story with her, she couldn't help being intrigued and interested. I showed Noelle the video footage with the phantom laughing, as well as the footage of Rus's strange behavior.

The day came and went without a supernatural incident, and Noelle fell asleep on the couch. I retired to my room with Rus. Noelle would later explain to me what she experienced that night.

That night, Noelle woke up to what she described as fingers being run through her hair. At first, she dismissed it as me playing a prank on her. She figured I had a video camera running and was trying to scare her for fun.

She remained still as her hair was stroked, until a raspy male voice whispered in her ear the word "hey." This was the same word said to me at Allen and Spencer's apartment. Part of me began believing that entity followed me. Another part of me dismissed it as coincidence.

Noelle jumped up from the couch and was surprised to see I wasn't standing there. She walked into my bedroom and saw me snoring away along with Rus. She returned to the couch, but not without pulling out her camera. Noelle started filming and asking questions quietly, hoping to receive an answer back. Unfortunately, nothing else was said.

Her experience was a little disturbing, considering the history of the house. Was the murdered rapist attempting to communicate with her? Was he trying to intimidate or re-create the crime he committed decades ago? I don't know. Needless to say it did not sit well with her. Noelle returned home the next day, and we all went about our business.

A few weeks later, I woke up around seven in the morning to use the bathroom. I was shocked to discover the front door of the house wide open. I immediately returned to my bedroom for a gun. I walked through the entire house and found no intruder of any kind.

This was really unsettling. If you knew me, you would know how attentive I am to keeping doors locked, especially at night. This led me to believe somebody else with a key entered the property. I immediately called Layne to see if possibly he had come in for one reason or another. He denied it, and reminded me that I had his copy of the key.

At the time I rented the property, he was about to leave town so he gave me his key to have a copy made. Hearing this from him did not make me feel any better. The door showed no signs of damage or breaking and entering. I had locked both the deadbolt and the doorknob lock, and latched the chain.

Even if someone had figured out a way to pick the locks, they could have never unlatched the chain without breaking the door. This told me that something from the inside opened the door.

It is kind of comical, really. I thought ghosts could walk through walls. I guess this one can't, or maybe he just prefers to use the door like he used to. I know Rus didn't open the door. I was a little surprised that Rus didn't bark and acknowledge the door opening to begin with, when it happened. He barked at every little sound there was in the past.

This occurrence caused me to wire my entire surveillance system throughout the house so it could document not only while I was there, but when I wasn't. Like the times before, the surveillance caught nothing, as the activity seemed to have stopped altogether.

A few more weeks passed and eventually I grew tired of watching uneventful surveillance footage. I did, however, capture the Internet technician who was there to fix a problem make himself a sandwich and drink a beer in my living room. I couldn't be there at the appointment, so I left the door unlocked for him. I figured that was an okay risk, considering I had surveillance cameras and Rus monitoring the property. But after finding nothing substantial to add to the already mysterious happenings, I dismantled the system and packed it away.

Months passed and the summer was nearly coming to a close. I was renting the place month-to-month, so I was not tied to a traditional lease. I decided to make plans and move further into North Carolina in September. I wasn't moving because of the previous activity. I was moving to be closer to members of my paranormal team and to be more available to clients I had been working with for years.

I made arrangements with Miss Iris Lennon to move into her Vintage Inn at the Squire's Inn. I had been researching that location for years and I couldn't think of a better place to live, for a while. I found the location a great backdrop and perfect for sitting and writing.

The added bonus, of course, was living on the property of a truly haunted location. As if I didn't have enough of that already, but it would give me the opportunity to continue my work there.

There were still a few weeks left of August at the house in Ocean Isle, and one night in particular would prove to be very intense. Layne had returned to take Rus with him, since he knew I would be moving soon. So at that point I was without my little watchdog buddy.

A few nights later, I was fast asleep in my room. I awoke abruptly to the sound of something falling somewhere in the house. I quickly leaped out of bed and went to investigate. It was dark and I could have kicked myself for not grabbing a flashlight.

In the middle of the floor was a ceramic statue of an angel that originally rested on the entertainment center. I could not for the life of me figure out what made it fall. I had been staying there for months and nothing like that happened before. Why fall now?

The statue fell five feet onto carpet. So I didn't expect it to be broken, and it wasn't. I even jumped up and down to see if I could shake the room enough to re-create the fall. I was unsuccessful.

Shortly after dismissing the falling statue, I returned to bed. That was when things escalated beyond my comfort zone. Once again, I heard something fall in the home. I ran back out into the living room to discover the same statue, nearly in the same spot on the floor. I had previously returned it to its original position on the entertainment center.

For a second time, I placed the statue back where it belonged. I couldn't help but echo the words of Layne, when he advised me to never move anything in the house. I was starting to think my ghost was back and doing this out of spite.

As I was about to return to bed, I heard a loud bang come from the guest room. I was startled, to say the least. I was a little smarter this time, and grabbed a night vision camera and a pistol from my bedroom. This way I could move through the house without giving away my location, but still see clearly. If there was an intruder, I would see them, but they would not be able to see me and they certainly wouldn't see a gun.

I investigated the guest room and found nothing. This was beyond ridiculous. All these phantom sounds as vivid as can be, yet nothing rational creating them. I was beginning to think I was going nuts. As I started to return to the bedroom the doorknob to the front door started to shake ever so slightly. It was turning left and right in a subtle fashion as if a person was attempting to open the door. My heart started racing and the nervousness in my stomach was overwhelming.

The thought of somebody trying to break into your home is absolutely terrifying. I realized my car was behind the house, so if somebody had been scouting my place, they would think I wasn't home, since I usually parked out front. I had parked out back because it was easier to load up boxes for the move.

I had no other choice but to believe somebody was trying to break into the house. However, the motion light on the porch was not on. How could a person get all the way up onto the porch and to the door, without setting it off? That light came off and on all the time at night from cats and the tree branches moving in the wind.

I lifted the pistol up toward the little window in the door to peer out through the curtain. That's when I realized the screen door was still closed. How was the doorknob turning with the screen door still closed? That was paranormal by every definition.

Still wanting to believe this was a living, breathing person, I yelled out that I had a gun and was about to shoot through the door. In my mind, I had been filming the entire incident so if this person persisted, I would have everything I needed on film to justify protecting myself. Moments after I threatened to shoot, the doorknob stopped turning.

I gathered myself, and opened the door with the pistol poised and ready. I slowly opened the screen door and waved the gun in front of the motion light. The light instantly came on, illuminating my entire porch and half of the yard. Nobody was there.

Why would a ghost be afraid of a gun? If I were to take the history of the location into account, that might make sense if I was, in fact, dealing with the murdered rapist. I sat on the couch in the living room for a few hours while keeping the video camera filming. The rest of the night remained quiet.

This just goes to show you that ghosts can appear anywhere and there doesn't necessarily have to be a tragic story attached. There doesn't have to be a creepy, old house involved either. Day or night, supernatural activity can happen anywhere at any time. Whether or not the same entity was following me around, the proof is there that wherever I go, I can't escape what I am destined to be.

A few days later, I officially moved from Ocean Isle to Warsaw, North Carolina, where I would once again find myself surrounded by the supernatural at the Squire's Inn.

SEVEN

Squire's Inn

It's not every night a ghost crawls into bed with you. That may sound silly, but I'm not kidding. But more on that a little later.

The night I moved into the Vintage Inn at the Squire's Inn, I had the most vivid dream. When I woke up from the dream I immediately wrote it down.

Occasionally, the air we breathe has a certain allure to it. Sometimes we discover a wind with a magical atmosphere that speaks volumes and tells a story all its own. Once in a while, there is a breeze with a crisp essence and a somewhat clean winter chill draped over its wings, that touches the skin like a butterfly kiss to deliver a message. Tonight I was surrounded by that feeling.

When I walked outside from the cottage, one thousand words were spoken to me from the tail end of a wispy kiss. Her touch acted as a prelude of the coming events and a blessing blanketed in a surreal mixture of divine intervention and spiritual awareness. The air I was breathing had a charming and mystical quality that I can hardly recall ever experiencing before.

The smell of the air was unique and intoxicating and almost indescribable. The cool October breeze made me feel like a child again, with a level of innocence, purity, and curiosity responding to every subtle touch of her breath. I was light-headed and felt as if I were floating in the haze of a lucid dream.

———————

Nightfall had welcomed her family of stars, and the eye of the night lit up the grounds with a cool hue of subtle blues. The atmosphere was tranquil and hypnotic, creating a world away from our world. For the moment, everything outside of the Squire was forgotten. There were no streets, towns or cities, no automobiles, cell phones, or televisions. Life had stood still.

———————

As I approached the courtyard, the moonlight brought the trees and statues to life. Everything around me felt alive. A faint pale blue mist weaved her fingers through the branches and wrapped her arms around the stone. The fountain glistened, bouncing shimmering rays of sparkling, almost metallic, light back at the moon as if they were waving to one another.

I stood frozen, lost in a spell cast by this enchanting abode. I was mesmerized by the rhythm and the somehow synchronized celebration of silhouettes. The leaves were swaying ever so slightly, and the flowers were dancing to an unheard melody orchestrated by the shadows.

My eyes began to focus on a large, framed, heavy wooden door, just beyond the courtyard. I could hear faint conversations beyond the wall of the Squire's Inn. I walked across the brick path, into the center of the courtyard, to be greeted and surrounded by at least a dozen shadows of men.

These were the knights of the Squire. They were the protectors of these grounds. The knights did not have any defining features. Their bodies were a heavy black outline of man filled with a solid black that had an original quality and color tone, nothing the living man could re-create. The knights were nothing, yet everything, at the same time. I stood in silence as they stared at me.

Fear never overcame my body during this standoff and inspection of one another. The knights and I were simply curious of the intentions of the other. After a few moments, two of the guardians stepped out of the stone path leading to the entrance of the Squire. I accepted this as their approval of my intentions.

I slowly walked past the knights, keeping my line of sight straight forward. I wanted to show respect and trust. During studies of Asian cultures, I learned that making eye contact is a sign of mistrust and a practice only left to those viewed as enemies. I have taken that philosophy and placed it into my own beliefs. I did not view the knights as enemies.

I continued on, gripped the large iron handle, and with both hands pulled open the door entering the Squire's Inn.

I stood inside the building on the other side of the door for a few moments, to completely digest what I had just witnessed. I started thinking that the Squire was some sort of gateway or spiritual magnet, or maybe even what could be perceived as a heaven. Even to myself I felt those thoughts were quite absurd, but the dead are out there and they are everywhere so it only made sense to me that there just might be a place or maybe more than one place that becomes their home in the afterlife.

A little bit more on the poetic side for me, I know. What was I to expect? I live my life chasing after testaments of the supernatural hoping to catch a glimpse of the afterlife. It makes sense I would be dreaming about it. But it was a dream inspired by my new home. I guess for that moment, I was allowed to write outside the realm of reality.

Now back to reality. Until this moment, my previous years of research at the Squire's Inn revealed supernatural activity deriving from a deceased little girl, around eleven years old. I have pictures of her in my possession.

In one photo, in the bottom left window of one of the buildings, you can see what appears to be a little girl peeking out. This is just one of many photographs taken with her presence in them. However, dozens of stories have been reported of not only witnessing a little girl, but also the original builder of the restaurant, Joseph West, and even former employees.

In addition to that, there was never much said about the inn portion of the property being haunted. A few stories were murmured here and there but nothing with any real substance. The majority of ghost sightings mostly focused on the Squire's Inn. All of that was about to change and I would soon discover more than just the ghost of a little girl.

I was residing in a room at the inn. I could not have asked for a better situation. My door opened up to a beautiful vineyard. Many days, I would sit in the vineyard simply to take in the atmosphere.

The room had three floor-to-ceiling windows, with heavy wooden shutters. With the shutters closed, the room would be pitch black. No light from outside could break through the shutters. I liked that. Room 26 was an all-open room. The bathroom was the only other area with a door. Even the mirror and sink were in the main living area.

A long wooden desk lined the wall adjacent to the bed. Vintage paintings graced the walls, and a small table sat nestled in the corner of the room. This place was literally a writer's cave. It was perfect for what I needed, which wasn't much.

I celebrated my thirty-fifth birthday on September 8. I brought in my team to celebrate by spending a few nights inside the Squire's Inn, conducting research. They were envious, to say the least, when I told them I was living there now. Not much happened that weekend in terms of locating the little girl spirit. But it was fun, regardless.

A few days later, I was returning to my room, after having dinner at the Squire Restaurant. When I entered my room, I noticed that the stained glass lamp hanging from the ceiling was on. At that moment, I recalled turning all the lights off when I left. I didn't think twice about it and brushed it off, as I perhaps forgot to turn it off.

That night, I was sitting at the table typing on my laptop, when I heard a very soft female voice say my name. All she said was "Stephen." I jerked my head in the direction the voice came from, but no one was there.

I thought possibly I was wrong, and the voice came from outside the windows. So I opened the shutters to see if anyone was outside. It would have been odd if there was, considering it was after midnight and the Squire Restaurant closed at nine o' clock.

I even considered that somebody was staying in one of the rooms next to me, and hearing my name was nothing more than coincidence. But I verified the following day with Miss Iris, and she said that I was the only one in the whole building.

During the fall and winter, the inn remained vacant for the most part, until the weekends. This was a weeknight, so it made sense nobody was renting a room. I shook off the voice and figured I was tired, and my mind was playing tricks on me. I shut down the laptop and decided to take a shower.

Following my shower, I was standing in front of the mirror. When I was looking at my reflection, I was forced to quickly perform a 180-degree turn when I saw a woman standing across the room, behind me.

Once my body came completely around, she was gone. I only caught a glimpse of her for a fraction of a second. But it was enough time for me to see her clearly enough to describe her.

She was blonde and tiny. I would say she was just shy of five feet tall. The woman was skinny and wearing a one-piece dress that appeared light gray to me. Now, I do suffer from a rare colorblindness that causes me to see colors differently than others, so I can't say for sure it was grey. If past mistakes have taught me anything, the dress was most likely light blue. I can't describe her face in detail, but I could tell she was in her mid-thirties.

I was pretty much chalking this sighting up to being tired, as well. So I decided to retire for the evening. As I started to fall asleep, I was glad that real or not, it wasn't what has possibly been following me. I fell asleep shortly after.

The next morning, I left for a drive into town to pick up a few supplies and to stop by Noelle's house. Noelle lived only twelve minutes or so away from the Squire's Inn. Upon arrival, I explained to her the experience of the previous night. I told her it very well could have all been in my mind. But considering the history of the location and the proof I already had in files about the little girl, it isn't that hard to believe that maybe there were others.

Noelle confided in me as well. She said strange things were beginning to happen in her home that reminded her of previous occurrences at other locations we were subjected to. She said she was getting the impression of an older male. The voices she was hearing sounded just like the male she heard at my home in Ocean Isle. Could he have followed her home instead of me? Like me, she was keeping an open eye with an open mind, and equipment to document close by. I left her house after a few hours, to return home.

Once again when I arrived at Room 26, the overhead light was on. At this point I was growing very suspicious. I left my room during the day, which meant no lights even needed to be on to begin with. So why, when I returned in the evening, was that light and only that light on?

I jumped in front of the laptop to add Noelle's experience in her home to my notes, for later reference. For a second time, I heard a female voice. This time she did not say my name. This time she simply sighed. It was a sigh of frustration. But frustrated by what? Maybe she was frustrated with me for not being able to hear her or respond accordingly. I don't know. Later that night, I would learn that her frustration was most likely due to loneliness.

The evening fell, and I had just finished up showering. The fan overhead in the bathroom was spinning and spinning and causing a great deal of noise contamination. But it was at that moment I heard the same female speak my name.

Of course, hundreds of thoughts shoot through your brain all at once during moments like this. There I was standing naked, dripping wet, and somebody in my room says my name. I mean in all reality, nobody never really considers a ghost at first. So, the possibility of an actual living person in my room was still the initial thought.

I wrapped a towel around myself and walked out of the bathroom. As you probably guessed, nobody was there. I walked over and turned on a high definition stereo camera that was installed on my computer, to begin documenting just in case something else happened. I continued getting dressed without interruption.

About an hour later, I walked over to the Squire's Inn to get a late bite to eat. As always, the staff there was asking me about any experiences I may have had since moving in. I kept quiet for the most part. I really did not want to say too much until I was certain a ghost was the culprit.

However, one waitress had a story to share. She told me the strangest feeling came over her the night before. She was closing up the restaurant and cleaning up in the tavern section of the building. There were only two employees scheduled to clean up and she was one of them.

The other employee was in the kitchen, washing pots and making all sorts of noise. That's when she heard a female talking just outside the tavern. The waitress was convinced a customer was still in the building. She walked out into the lobby and discovered the main entrance was still locked, and nobody was in sight. To the right of her, she briefly caught a glimpse of a woman entering the wine tasting area.

The waitress quickly followed, but no person was found. She informed the other employee that somebody was still left in the building. They both walked through the entire restaurant in search of the late night straggler.

After completing a sweep of the restaurant, they both verified that every entrance into the building was still in the locked position. No person could have left without leaving the door unlocked unless they had a key. The two employees finally gave up and jokingly dismissed it as the Squire's ghost. They closed up and left for the night.

After her story and the filling of my belly, I returned to my room for the remainder of the night. I was surprised when I entered my room and discovered my computer had shut down and the camera was powered off. The computer shutting down could have been a result of the power going off briefly, but I didn't recall the lights flickering throughout the property while I was eating.

I powered the computer back up to check the footage captured by the camera from the point I went to eat, to the point the computer powered off. I watched about ninety minutes of footage before the camera powered off. According to the time stamp, the computer and camera had turned off just moments before I returned to my room.

Could have been coincidence, I suppose. But I couldn't help but think the spirit was near and she might have pulled the energy from the electronics to do something. At this point, I was trying to figure out what that something was going to be.

I set the camera to begin recording again, and luckily moments after doing so, the bathroom light started to flicker. As I sat in the chair, my stomach turned to knots when I started to hear a creaking coming from the bathroom.

I turned to look and witnessed the bathroom door slowly begin to close. I jumped up and grabbed a handheld video camera. I powered it on, and hit record in just enough time to catch the last second of the door closing. I immediately opened the door, with the camera still recording, to document nobody had been on the other side.

At this point, I was convinced something could see me but I could not see it. I was also considering the possibility that if it was this woman I had been witnessing, she could be aware of the cameras.

I called Noelle, since I knew she would still be awake. I asked her to come over to take a look at the footage. She arrived about twenty minutes later, and I showed her the door closing and described all the recent activity. Noelle was sitting on the bed while I was playing the recordings through the computer.

Without warning, the computer powered off again. This time Noelle was able to witness it, and this time it powered back on. But it did not load up normally. The computer simply loaded to a black screen.

I thought the computer had crashed and that was the end of it. But as I was in the middle of that thought, the bathroom door started closing again. Noelle jumped up and ran to the door. She examined it inside and out, and even tried multiple times to re-create the door closing. I assured her that other than earlier that evening, the door never once did that. The hinges are stiff and even if you push the door with force, it catches and stops half way to closing.

At this point, we were both standing just outside the bathroom when my computer shut off again. This time it loaded back up normally. That was when I noticed something moving at the bottom of the bed. I pointed and gathered Noelle's attention so she could see it. I grabbed the handheld video camera and started recording.

The blankets were moving ever so slightly toward the bottom of the bed. We both felt this could be normal, that the weight of the blankets simply caused them to slip. I turned off the video camera and we sat in the room discussing everything up until this point. As we were having the conversation, I was glancing over the video footage of the blankets moving.

That's when I noticed something neither one of us noted at the time. There was a solid black shadow about two-and-a-half feet long and one foot wide at the foot of the bed. We never thought anything of it at the time because there were plenty of shadows cast throughout the room, so it didn't stand out.

But then, it moved. In a split second, the shadow slid from the foot of the bed to the floor and then was gone. This was pretty incredible. But as always, Noelle and I tried to re-create it. We grabbed the camera and stood in the same exact spots we were standing earlier, just outside the bathroom. We re-created the incident exactly while recording video.

Shortly after our experiment, we reviewed the footage and the shadow was not there. During our experiment I even waved my hands up and down and all around trying to cast shadows. Nothing came close to looking like what was filmed prior.

Looking back on this now, I consider that entire experience to be a prelude. Noelle left for the evening, and I locked the door behind her. I powered my handheld camera off and placed it on the table, leaving the camera connected to the computer running.

It was well after midnight and I decided since the door was the last piece of activity to occur, I would retire for the night. I turned off all the lights and the computer monitor then crawled into bed.

As I started dozing off, my senses were startled by a quick popping sound and something mechanical powering down. Glancing across the room I noticed there weren't any lights coming from the computer or the camera.

Once again, the computer and camera had turned off, without human intervention. Maybe my computer was malfunctioning and simply needed repair. But why would an independent camera suffer the same symptoms simultaneously? I considered a faulty outlet as well.

I continued staring off into the room before finally falling to sleep. Hours later the unthinkable occurred.

I was lying on my side asleep when the bed started to move ever so slightly. The movement was subtle, yet enough to wake me. I continued to lie still. We have all been there. We have all experienced that well-known half-asleep, barely-awake state of mind. Was I dreaming or was I experiencing reality?

Suddenly, somebody crawled into bed right up behind me. The feeling was so vivid and undeniably felt just like when a person enters the bed. The bed sunk toward the person and the blankets lifted. At first, in my sleepy state, I dismissed it as my girlfriend crawling into bed with me, so I started dozing back off.

Then like a flash of lightning, my eyes opened wide and those knots returned in my stomach. I realized so much within seconds. My girlfriend was at her house. I was the only one with a key to the room. The door was locked at the knob, locked at the deadbolt, and chained at the top. Somebody was directly behind me in the bed, and I had no clue who it was.

Just as all of these realizations struck me, the woman breathed out a sigh of relief just inches from my ear. I leaped from the bed and fell onto the wooden floor. I jumped up to only slip and fall again. I finally made it to the light switch and turned it on. I was shaking my head in disbelief at the sight of an empty bed.

I quickly grabbed an electromagnetic field tester and placed it on the area in question. At first, the reads were high, peaking at seventy on the Gauss scale. But as quick as it was there it was gone, returning to low, standard, and expected reads.

I have seen and heard many crazy things throughout my life. I have been attacked. Objects have been thrown at me. But never before has a ghost crawled into bed with me. Maybe I reminded her of someone. Maybe I was just convenient. Maybe as I suggested before, she was lonely.

I don't know, but either way, I will never be convinced otherwise. The female spirit went out of her way to get my attention over and over, until finally crossing that line approaching full body contact.

That experience was unnerving. When she sighed in my ear, I felt a soft, bitter cold that sent chills down my spine. It was so real. There isn't a single person out there that would have not believed somebody living had entered that bed.

I didn't know what to say as I stood dumbfounded in my room. I wasn't sure how to feel. Part of me felt sympathy, while other parts of me felt disturbed and confused. I never went back to sleep that night. As soon as the sun came up I walked out to the vineyard to clear my head. I kept looking back at the room wondering what the story was with this woman. Who was she looking for? Why was she communicating with me? What did she want to say?

EIGHT

The Mirror
Never Lies

U DIE U might have well been referring to the demise of the P.I.T. Crew. It was around this time that my head investigator and I decided to close the chapter on the team, to pursue individual research.

This was not an easy decision to reach. However, ever since the Eidolon case, the team was never the same. We fought over the most ridiculous things. Hate began to overpower all of us. The word "drama" was never tied to my team. No way. But something happened that made our inner strength, friendship, relationships, and work ethics crumble.

I also feared that this lifestyle was overcoming some of us in a very dangerous way. It was time to bow out. Some of the members took this very hard, while others welcomed the change. To me it was like watching your family die. The P.I.T. Crew was my baby, and we all went through so much and discovered some amazing things.

I left open to all former members the option of calling one another, if ever needed for an individual case. So a few of us kept a tight bond and continued working without the brand name. However, mirrors can tell a story and the chapters in those stories change.

I am certain you have heard, at one point or another, of people witnessing spirits within mirrors. Whether they saw a face or a full-body apparition, the stories are endless. I have even heard reports of messages seen written within mirrors.

Over the years, I have experienced all of this as well. In fact, one of the most credible photographs of a ghost I had ever taken was one staring back at me from within a mirror. I captured that picture at the Brentwood Wine Bistro, in Little River, South Carolina, years ago. That photograph gained worldwide attention and has been seen on various network programs about the paranormal.

There was an older gentleman staring right back at me, from the upper right hand corner of the mirror. The photograph was captivating and thought provoking, to say the least, and also highly criticized. But criticism comes with the territory. It is a necessary evil. That picture was not the last time I dealt with a ghost in a mirror. The most recent experience started with a phone call from Noelle.

A few weeks after my phantom bed raider experience, Noelle called me in a panic. She was hoping to gain comfort from me, in hopes of hearing that a clever prank had been pulled. That was not the case, however. Again, this is one of those scenarios when you find yourself thinking rationally and keeping your thoughts well within the realm of reality.

Noelle lived tucked away surrounded by trees down a long dirt road about twelve minutes from my room at the Squire's Inn. At the time of the incident, she was home alone, and I had not been there in days.

I could tell by the tone of her voice that she was really shaken up and concerned that somebody had been in her home recently. She told me that following a shower the words "I know" appeared to be written on her bathroom mirror. This obviously startled her and she immediately ran through the house searching for a living and breathing culprit. But she found no one.

As cliché as it sounds, "I know" was there and in plain sight. She immediately took a photograph of the writing before the fogged-up mirror began to fade. Noelle wasn't thinking supernatural at all. At first she thought an intruder had been in her home or that I had played a prank.

However, as I said to her, even if I had written that message on her mirror days prior, it would have never had such clarity days later. Never mind the fact that she had taken a shower every day since my last visit and never noticed it before. Something like that does not go without noticing.

She assured me her doors had been locked, including the door to the bathroom.

I immediately drove over to her house with some of my equipment used for paranormal research. Where Noelle was thinking physical intruder, I was thinking spiritual intruder. Of course by the time of my arrival, the message was gone. But she did have the pictures to show me.

I couldn't help but laugh a little considering how cliché the message was. I made a few horror movie jokes in an attempt to lighten the mood, but that only seemed to make Noelle's anxiety about the situation worse.

I stayed that night in hopes of witnessing the supernatural. I set up a few video cameras and kept my meters for measuring electromagnetic fields, ionic energy, and temperature near the couch I was going to sleep on. I wanted to be prepared. Unfortunately, nothing happened at all.

I left the next morning while Noelle was calling around asking potential suspects about what she still believed to be a prank. At the time, the only other person to have a key to her house was her sister Joey. It wasn't hard to fathom the idea that she came into the house and popped open the bathroom door while Noelle was showering.

The lock on the bathroom door was simple. Any little long piece of metal could be placed through the hole in the doorknob to pop open the lock. I'm guessing that was a child safety feature. But Noelle's interrogating prompted no concrete answers as to what happened.

I know Joey personally, and a poker face isn't something she has. If she had pulled a prank, the beans would have been spilled almost instantly. So, I found myself still rooted in the belief something spiritual had taken place. A few nights later, Noelle had a more eye opening experience.

It was late that night, and she had retired to the bedroom and was unwinding to entertainment from her laptop computer. All of a sudden her entire house shook as if an earthquake was taking place. The shaking was brief and over within seconds. Just moments before the house started shaking, a loud crashing sound came from outside. She described it to me like something very large had hit the side of her home. Imagine a truck driving full speed into the side of your house, and I think you will understand the impact that had taken place.

Strangely, nothing had hit the side of Noelle's house. Further investigation revealed no earthquake or anything remotely related happening in the nearby area that could have caused her entire home to shake.

She immediately started filming with a video camera, just in case it happened again or something else occurred. During filming she captured a male's voice. The voice was subtle and almost inaudible. It was hard to understand what was being said, but there was no denying a man had said something. What was spoken remained a mystery.

The next evening, I visited Noelle again in hopes of witnessing some of the phenomena. Once again, I was planning on spending the entire night monitoring her home.

This proved to be quite difficult because at the time, her three children were in the house. Neither one of us wanted to scare them by explaining what I was doing with all of those neat "toys," so we kept my visit ambiguous.

Noelle's children at the time were ages five, seven, and ten, with the youngest being a girl. Her children know me as "Indy." To them I am the ghost guy always on some sort of adventure, so they are well aware of what I do. Occasionally, her children bomb me with questions about ghosts and I always keep my answers honest and full of tact.

With their mother actively involved in the field of paranormal research and "Indy" always being around, a child's curiosity will always prevail. The stereotypical American family doesn't often include a handful of ghosts, so I imagine her children feel like they are in a unique and fun situation. They call my car the "ghost mobile." Enough said.

That evening, Noelle's middle child, Tanner, appeared to be attached to me. He was following me all through the house, no matter what I was doing. It was like he wanted to tell me something or ask me something, but couldn't bring himself to do it.

At eight in the evening, the children were sent to their rooms for bed. Tanner insisted on sleeping in the living room on the couch and his mother allowed him to do it. I decided to sit in the living room as well while Noelle retired to her bedroom for the evening.

Tanner refused to go to sleep, so I sat beside him on the couch hoping I could get him to talk a little. Inside, I had a hunch there was something bothering him. As we were sitting on the couch, a loud crashing sound startled the both of us. The sound came from the kitchen. Both of our heads jerked instantly toward the direction of the sound. The living room and kitchen are adjoined, so we had a perfect line of sight from the couch.

I chuckled to myself as I watched Tanner stare into the kitchen. I could tell in his head he was trying to make sense of what had just happened. Nothing was on the kitchen floor and nothing was out of place to justify the crashing sound we both heard.

Tanner immediately started scanning the living room. He pointed out the household cat sitting quietly on the chair adjacent to us. He even made it a point to tell me that the sound could not have come from the cat, since she was sitting right in front of us. I admired the deduction skills coming from a seven-year-old. His mother must have been rubbing off on him.

Tanner looked at me and asked if I had heard the crashing sound, and I told him I did. I asked him what he thought it was and he looked up at me and said, "A ghost." I asked him if he was sure and he said, "Indy, I'm starting to think ghosts are real." I told him that maybe they were.

Shortly after the phantom crashing sound, I told Tanner to try to get some sleep. I was going to take a quick shower before sitting up any longer. What happened next was show-stopping incredible.

As planned I took my shower at Noelle's house. I locked myself in the bathroom to prevent one of the children from barging in. It was a typical shower. I'm hoping many of you know the steps and process well. The bathroom filled with steam. Naked paranormal investigator in, followed by naked paranormal investigator out.

I opened the curtain and exited the shower, and like most of us do, I wrapped a towel around me. I walked over to the sink, which of course was underneath the infamous all-knowing mirror. I stopped dead in my tracks. I could not believe what I was seeing.

Three tiny hand prints were firmly planted near the top of the foggy mirror. They looked just like a toddler's handprint. If I were to guess, I would say a two- or three-year-old would had to have done that. I immediately grabbed my cell phone and started snapping pictures, but the fog on my lens resulted in less than perfect images.

I stared at the mirror for a few moments examining the prints. The detail was astounding. I could even see the tiny lines of the skin imprinted on the mirror. The one handprint was really defined, while the other two more or less looked like hand smears.

I grabbed the door knob, just to make sure I had in fact locked the door before showering. The door was still locked. I experimented with an idea really quickly.

I turned the shower back on, closed the curtain, and then I opened the bathroom door. Upon doing so, the curtain to the shower blew inward, creating a ripple effect. If that door had been opened while I was showering, the curtain would have been blown toward me from the air flow, and that would not have gone without noticing.

I quickly threw on some clothes and ran to Noelle's room. Luckily she was still awake. Young Tanner was, too. I asked Noelle to come to the bathroom with me, but to make sure Tanner stayed in the living room.

Excited and curious to see what I was raving about, she followed me to the bathroom. I walked in and pointed to the mirror. Luckily the fog was present and the little hand-prints were still quite visible. Noelle immediately yelled for Tanner to come to the bathroom and he did.

She asked him if he had done this while "Indy" was showering and he said no. I interrupted the interrogation to put out that the door was locked and I tested the effects of the door opening while showering. I assured Noelle that nobody came through that door.

The next thing I knew, her daughter LaeSea had awoke from all of the commotion. She quickly ran to the bathroom to see what all of the excitement was about. Noelle had to ask if she was responsible for the phantom hand-prints. Of course LaeSea said no.

The children both seemed so intrigued by this and of course the questions were flying. LaeSea kept asking, "Who did that? What did that?" Her questions were followed by infectious laughter. These kids were nonstop, I tell you. You would think children of that age would be scared of a ghost. But, no this crowd was much different and I loved it.

The four of us stood there staring at the mirror, trying to arrive at a believable conclusion. But nothing was making sense. So for the sake of more deduction I asked Tanner to reach up across the sink as far as he could and place his hand on the mirror. He could barely reach the middle of the mirror upon doing so.

LaeSea was even shorter than he was, but I had her do the same thing. She could not even reach the mirror from across the sink. So Noelle held her daughter up and LaeSea placed her print on the mirror.

Interesting enough, with the two children placing their own handprints on the mirror, this gave Noelle and me something to compare to. Their handprints were not even remotely close in size to the tiny prints at the top of the mirror. Both Noelle and I knew we did not even need to ask her oldest son, Gabriel. His handprints would have been even bigger than the younger two.

After standing in silence for a few moments, Noelle instructed her children to go back to bed. They of course fought the notion, because now there was some ghostly excitement going on. I can't blame them.

Eventually the handprints faded away as the fog on the mirror evaporated. Noelle and I started discussing alternate possibilities by comparing all that had happened in the past. Whatever was happening to all of us seemed to be related.

Someone or something wrote on her mirror with a clear message. They knew something. Then I experienced three tiny handprints on the same mirror. Couple that with the other strange occurrences at her house and you might call that a haunting. But I don't understand why or how.

Could we have been magnetized due to all of the spiritual energy we had exposed ourselves to? Are we drawing these spirits to us, or are they attaching themselves without an invitation? There are too many questions without answers.

The rest of the night was quiet. Eventually everybody including myself was fast asleep. The next morning arrived with Noelle and me both mutually agreeing that with this activity hitting home, we both needed a vacation. Now, that was an idea I could reflect on.

NINE

The Bluethenthal Mansion

"No rest for the wicked," or so they say. I prefer to say, "The wicked won't let me rest," courtesy of the mysterious and unpredictable Bluethenthal Mansion.

A relaxing weekend away from everything with my girlfriend at a gorgeous bed-and-breakfast in Wilmington, North Carolina, drastically changed at the mention of that cursed word, "ghost." Damn that word. I just can't get away from it. This is my destiny, and that fact appears to be proven over and over.

Of course when it comes to the supernatural and all things it encompasses, how could I say no to a murder, suicides, a secret passageway, a burning church, and a bizarre room believed to have been designed for private orgies?

I couldn't say no. Neither could my girlfriend, Noelle, for that matter. In fact, she would have been pushing me out of the way and running right at such a story if I had declined what was offered to us.

When we arrived in Wilmington that Friday evening, neither one of us expected what would transpire after a night inside the mansion. We pulled up to this colossal building at six-thirty in the evening. I was impressed, to say the least.

I knocked on the door, and a very tall Greek man answered, in a very welcoming fashion. His name was Chris, and he wasted no time offering me beer, wine, food, and help with our luggage. He had me at beer, but ultimately both he and his wife would be feeding Noelle and me much in the caffeine department.

Noelle waited in the car while Chris escorted me to the attic suite. I was overwhelmed by the grandeur of this mansion. The antiques and restored beauty of the early 1900s shined through. I felt like I was in a museum. I did not want to touch anything.

I like my privacy. I especially enjoy my privacy when I am attempting to escape the paranormal world and enjoy time with Noelle. So I booked us the attic suite, which is referred to as the "Madison Room."

The Madison Room is the only suite offered in the mansion. It is a very spacious room with a private bath, a fireplace, and honestly, some rather creepy décor. I believe the wooden teddy bear nestled in a crib took the cake for the both of us.

In fact, it really seemed out of place. I have to admit, the room gave me an overall feeling of staying at grandma's house. I am sure many can relate to that and understand exactly what I am saying.

After Chris showed me the suite, I quickly ran out of the building to let Noelle know the arrangements had been made. I could not wait for her to see the room, and I had to mention to her how creepy parts of the home were. What did you expect?

Noelle and I hauled our luggage up three levels and finally unloaded everything in our suite. About an hour later, Noelle was sitting by the window, staring down at the gardens below. I was sitting in one of the chairs, attempting to find something interesting to watch on cable television. Truth be told, I wasn't having much success.

Out of the blue, Noelle commented on seeing something that was plain weird. As she was staring out the window, she witnessed a tall man in a trench coat and fedora walk through the gardens. She described him as looking like he just walked out of the 1930s. He walked directly behind a large oak tree. Noelle kept staring and waiting for him to continue walking, but he never did. The strange man seemed to disappear behind the tree. Of course, neither one of us were thinking on a paranormal level at that point.

A few hours later as we were continuing to relax, something occurred that startled both of us. One of the walls had a removable panel that allowed access to the crawl spaces throughout the roof. This access panel blended in perfectly with the rest of the wall. Neither one of us would have ever discovered the panel if it had not opened on its own.

As we were standing in the middle of the Madison Room, the panel flew off of the wall and hit a nearby dresser causing a loud banging sound. Of course we both jumped at the surprise, and then laughed it off.

Again, we were not thinking anything paranormal. We simply dismissed the panel opening as a result of us walking around the room and causing vibrations. Noelle made a joke following this, suggesting that the fireplace in the room was a secret passageway.

The next morning, we were planning on hitting the town of Wilmington. We walked down through the amazing mansion, and attempted to creep past the dining room on the first floor where other guests were enjoying an excellent breakfast. Neither one of us was really interested in breakfast.

That was when Angie, a very nice and eclectic lady—and wife to Chris—stopped us. She was the owner of the old Bluethenthal Mansion, turned Angie's Bed and Breakfast.

She of course invited us to breakfast, but all we could insist on was coffee. Angie wanted to make sure our stay was perfect. Believe me when I tell you this lady was the perfect host. Angie asked us how our first night in the building was. This prompted Noelle to ask her about the man she saw walking outside and disappearing behind a tree the night before. Angie wasted no time laughing and simply said, "Oh that's just our ghost." There's the damn word neither one of us could resist.

She continued by describing what he looks like, and where he can often be seen in the house. Angie said he likes to walk from the kitchen and into the living room, then outside into the gardens. I was amazed. Angie described the mysterious man exactly how Noelle had described him to me the night before. What really impressed me was the fact that Noelle had no prior knowledge of this guy. You just can't call something like that coincidence.

I then proceeded to introduce myself as an author and paranormal researcher. Noelle did the same. Angie was delighted and tickled to have actual paranormal investigators in her home. She asked us if we would investigate the ghosts that haunt the mansion and try to get her visual proof. Luckily for her and us, Noelle and I always traveled with our equipment so we, of course, said yes. We were there for the weekend and simply could not pass up such a unique opportunity.

But something Angie said prompted me to inquire as to why she said "ghosts," plural. Angie responded by saying there was also a female spirit who resided there. She also said it didn't matter if we found anything or not, she believed them to be there and very real.

I told Angie we would need to interview her fully, prior to investigating. We set up a time in the early afternoon to do just that. She also said we could have the run of the place after nightfall. The building was going to be ours to explore.

Angie needed to finish up entertaining her other guests, so we went ahead into downtown Wilmington for the morning.

Noelle and I returned early afternoon armed with our cameras to interview Angie.

We met in the living room, surrounded by gorgeous vintage furniture, paintings, and artifacts. Before interviewing her, Angie gave us a tour of the property. The house was so full of unique little nuances.

For one, underneath the rug in the dining room was a button that could be pushed by your foot. That button caused a trap door in the ceiling to open. That was so neat. All of the walls held old photographs that tied to the history of the property and the souls that once inhabited it. The mansion was full of history.

I stationed a camera on Angie as she sat on one of the couches. She began to tell her story. The area surrounding the old mansion seemed to have a curse on it. Angie told us stories of a once-neighboring church that ended in death and a catastrophic fire. The priest of the church had gone away on a mission. He left the church in the hands of one of his nuns. Unfortunately, for whatever reason, she suffered from a terrible fall down the stairs inside. She remained on the floor in pain for one week, until the priest returned. After discovering her, she died in his arms.

Shortly after the nun's death, a fire with no known origin burned the church to the ground. The fire was so hot and blazing that it caught the side of the Bluethenthal Mansion on fire. Pictures of the infamous fire can be seen hanging inside Angie's Bed and Breakfast. The fire caused the mansion to be uninhabitable.

Years would pass before Angie and Chris would come along, making an offer on the home. Nobody wanted it prior to them, considering all of the damage and renovation that would need to take place.

Shortly after they acquired the home both Angie and Chris started to experience strange occurrences in the building. As she described to us before, sightings of the infamous fedora man were becoming the norm.

But it wasn't until the discovery of a murdered woman that the haunting activity rose to an all-time high. Angie told us the true story of a woman who was murdered by her husband. The woman apparently wanted to leave her husband, so she threw him out of the house. He broke in one night with a gun and shot his wife. She fell back onto a large wooden desk. As she attempted to call emergency services, he kept firing the gun off at her. She died shortly after, draped across her desk.

Angie said this lady's furniture went up for auction and much of it sold. However, nobody would buy the desk because it had such a bad flavor to it. Angie purchased the desk for the bed-and-breakfast's office. Little did I know until then, Noelle and I had walked passed that desk a dozen times.

Angie continued with her stories and shared many guest experiences, too. They all seemed very similar. They ranged from witnessing the mystery man, as Noelle did, to hearing music, female cries, and footsteps. Nothing was ever reported to be violent. She said the activity just had a supernatural and creepy feeling to it, considering all the dark history of the property.

Angie described an instance with her husband, when he was sleeping. Chris was awakened one night, when the sheets he was sleeping under were slowly being pulled to the bottom of the bed. He quickly realized it wasn't Angie, but did claim to see a woman standing at the foot of the bed. This experience coupled, with many others, prompted Chris to push Angie to bring in a Catholic priest for an exorcism. However, she quickly talked him out of it.

Angie also described often hearing light music on the second floor. She heard it so many times, she memorized the melody. She hummed it to us. She then pointed out a few secrets of the house. Angie said in the room where we were staying, there was a secret passageway behind the fireplace.

She said that although she has never been in the room behind the fireplace, her husband had been once or twice, just to see what it was. To begin with, it was rather unique that a fireplace would even be in an attic, let alone with another entirely huge room behind it. I of course had to smirk at Noelle, considering she joked about the fireplace being a secret passageway the night before.

After the interview, with hours to wait until dark, Noelle and I decided to investigate our room and this intriguing fireplace. We grabbed a few cameras and a few lights and started examining the fireplace. Sure enough, there was a wooden panel in the back of the fireplace. Upon closer observation, we noticed handles attached to the panel. We would have never noticed this if Angie had not mentioned it. In fact, another observation showed that the fireplace was never even operable, so in a way it was fake. I reached back and pulled on the handles, and the panel slid toward me and out from under the brick.

We shined our lights through the newly discovered entrance to find a colossal, empty room with a few unique exceptions. In the center of the room was another room. However, this room had a little roof on it. The room was about the size of an average storage shed. It seemed so out of place.

After a few Scooby Doo and Hardy Boys jokes, we crawled through the entrance and started investigating the forgotten area. I noticed toward the left of the room were old gears, pulleys, and cranks that apparently at one time or another operated one of the first styles of elevators. Apparently, during reconstruction after the fire, the elevator was forgotten about and completely built around.

Noelle and I entered the little room within the big room. Inside, it looked like a huge walk-in closet. A few pieces of vintage ladies' lingerie still hung from old clothes hangers. We both looked at each other, puzzled. What would be the point of hiding a room inside a room full of ladies' lingerie? We both joked that it must have been a secret sex room.

Noelle scanned the area with a UV light commonly used by forensics teams to find blood samples, or other substances that may help solve a case. She discovered a substance across much of the floor. I will allow your imagination to run wild with that one. It could have been blood, or it could have been something else. We had no way to determine which.

The room itself had a chill factor to it. When we first entered, it was extremely hot. But as we continued finding clues about the origins of this room, the colder the air around us became. We crawled back through the fireplace to ponder everything we had heard and seen so far.

Shortly after, I noticed a door on the opposite side of our room we had yet to explore. The door was locked. I walked downstairs to ask Angie about it and she said it was another whole section of the attic. She gave us the key.

Noelle and I entered the other part of the attic. Our room, the Madison, was directly in between the secret part of the attic and now this newly found section. There wasn't much in this new section. It was fairly wide open.

While we were in the third section of the attic, I could faintly hear what sounded like a radio coming from behind us. I walked out and back into our room. I found one of our radios on the bed broadcasting white noise or static. Who turned it on? It wasn't one of us.

While I was examining the radio, a large thud hit the roof above the section Noelle was still investigating. This surprised her so much, that she bolted out of that area without looking back.

We were on the third floor and nothing was above that roof. There was especially nothing of such large size to fall and cause such a loud and demanding sound. It certainly was not a squirrel. The mysteries kept coming.

Noelle and I decided to keep investigating the attic areas. We found old newspaper articles with headlines revolving around multiple suicide jumpers from the roof. This story just kept getting more interesting.

Hours passed, and we decided to start creeping through the rest of the house. Our first stop was the living room where we interviewed Angie. The first thing that grabbed my attention was how significantly colder it was in that room. I even said to Noelle that my temperature gun was getting reads that should not have been. The reads were claiming it was below thirty degrees in there, yet the thermostats on the wall said differently. The thermostats stated it was seventy-three degrees in the room.

We went into the office with the infamous desk. The magnetic fields emitting from the desk were quite impressive. Wood is not a conductor, yet this desk was giving off more electromagnetic fields than a standard household refrigerator.

Noelle decided to sit in the dining room, while I was planning on returning to the Madison Room. As I reached the second level I could very faintly hear what was best described as a music box. The music was coming from the end of a long hall, which led to two guest rooms. Nobody was currently staying in those rooms. There was no sign of a machine or other device that could be making that music. This was exactly the melody that Angie hummed to me when she described hearing phantom music on the second floor.

I continued to the Madison Room and sat down on the bed for a minute. Within no time, I heard a male voice say, "I don't think he can hear it." I of course jerked my head in the direction of the sound and it was coming from the center of the room. One more time I heard, "I don't think he can hear it."

My eyes focused further across the room to my cell phone on the window sill. I realized I had not checked my phone in hours, and it was placed on silent since we were investigating. I walked over and grabbed my phone. On the screen it said, "One Missed Call." The call just happened. I fell back into one of the chairs and just started chuckling. First I hear a voice infer twice that I couldn't hear something, and then I discover at that very moment I was missing a phone call. That was bizarre to say the least.

Meanwhile, down in the dining room Noelle was about to capture something very remarkable. She was sitting at the dining room table asking questions, in hopes of getting a response. Noelle was asking questions about who lived there and what their purpose was. But it wasn't until she asked if the spirit residing there was the woman who was murdered, when something amazing happened.

Following that question, the sound of a gunshot echoed through the room. Noelle immediately paused and then with a shaky voice to the camera she said, "That sounded like a shot." This reminded me of course of the gunshot we heard at the hotel the night before we investigated the Piper Room. Was that experience some form of clairvoyance?

Was the experience at the hotel a prelude to finding this unique place and discovering another story full of ghosts? Those questions really make you wonder.

Noelle and I regrouped in the Madison Room to discuss our findings. She was excited, to say the least, concerning the gunshot. I heard it plain as day on her video. Now, there is nothing saying that something outside of the home didn't make the sound. Maybe it was a car backfiring. The old house does have a lot of echo. But when considering the story at hand, it's hard to say. That was certainly perfect timing on her part. The rest of the night went without incident.

The following morning, we met with Angie to discuss our findings. We could only show her what we knew of immediately. The rest would have to be reviewed, before knowing for sure. But she was delighted, to say the least. She lit up at the fact we shared in her experiences and none of this was even supposed to happen.

Our vacation destination had turned into an investigation of a place full of mystery and rich stories. Angie wasted no time inviting us to return for a weekend. There is certainly enough there that went unexplained to warrant such a visit. But maybe I will go back to finally get that vacation.

TEN

Josef's

They say, "X marks the spot." I rarely find that to be true in the field of paranormal research, when there are too many spots and not enough Xs. However, fate has a way of placing you in the right place at the right time, occasionally.

Behind the Squire's Inn & Vineyard in Warsaw, North Carolina, stands an old tobacco barn nicknamed the "But & Ben." According to Miss Iris Lennon, the owner of the property, the building acquired that name after it was converted into living quarters. She told me in her native Scotland, small living quarters consisting of a kitchen and one bedroom were considered to be a But & Ben.

Luckily for me, the historic structure was available for rent. I moved in over Labor Day weekend, 2013. I had fallen in love with the area and the Squire's Inn during my stay at the inn, and to be privileged enough to relocate back onto the property was an absolute treat. Not long after relocating, I also learned that the old tobacco barn converted into living quarters was the very first building ever constructed on the property, over one hundred years ago.

During my research at the Inn over a year prior, I learned that Joseph West also operated another restaurant called Josef's, up until he died in the early 1990s. Little did I know how close I was to making yet another discovery that seemingly appeared to be related to previous experience. I knew Joseph, whom most people called Joe, had owned another restaurant; I just wasn't sure of the exact location.

In the evenings, I would sit on my back porch, marveling at the architecture of a magnificent and haunting building, just beyond the tree line of my yard. This house was directly behind the guest houses of the Squire's Inn. The design of the home showed similarities to designs used in the structure at the Squire's Inn, so I often wondered if it was related in some way.

I started to notice no life seemed to be present. I never saw anybody going in or out, or vehicles in the driveway. Curiosity struck, so I investigated the outer portion of the home just to see if it was inhabited or not.

Upon a closer look, the home appeared to be vacant. I did notice a handicap parking sign, which led me to believe that the building served as some sort of business at some point in time. This prompted me to start asking the employees of the Squire's Inn about the empty structure nestled so closely to their property. I was informed that it was the former Josef's Restaurant, operated by the late Joseph West.

I couldn't believe that this astounding building was just sitting there empty. But with that being said, I knew I had to get in there to see if there was any relation to the haunting at the Squire's Inn. If Joe was in fact one of the many spirits at the Squire's Inn, it would only make sense that he could be haunting the grounds of his second restaurant as well.

I just needed to get inside of Josef's to see for myself. But before I did, I needed to conduct a little more research on the history. I wanted to know what I could possibly be getting myself and others into.

Over the course of the next few months, I started asking around town about Joe West and his former restaurants. I already knew a great deal about the history of the Squire's Inn, but Josef's was a bit more ambiguous.

A woman on the town commission informed me that shortly after Joe died, the restaurant exchanged hands. However, hard times and dark rumors forced the reopened restaurant to fail. She also informed me that the historic building was originally moved from a location about three miles away, to its current resting place.

A quick phone call to the gentleman who took over the property informed me that every employee working at that time never liked being in the building. He told me they all felt uneasy, and in the evenings, when shutting down for the night, not a single employee would walk through the house alone. They walked in pairs.

Of course at this point, I was more than biting at the bit to get into this place. For me, my research was expanding and to discover yet another tie to the Squire's Inn and to Joe West was more than exciting.

Shortly after, I inquired with Miss Iris about gaining permission to conduct research in the former Josef's. I knew if anybody could get me in there, it would be the person who purchased the Squire's Inn after Joe left it. A quick phone call on her part placed the key to the property in my hand.

I contacted Noelle Harper and Allen Bess. Both were trusted fellow researchers, and of course, at one point in time they were a part of my paranormal investigation team. They are two of the best whom I consistently work with. We set a weekend aside almost immediately to begin work. Allen and Noelle met at my house on Friday, November 8, 2013.

We began preparing all of the equipment and discussing the upcoming case. Around seven in the evening we made our way to the target. Just driving up to this house brought a level of intimidation. I'm not sure why. Call it a feeling, if you will. At this point, I call it a prelude.

Noelle started snapping pictures as we walked around the exterior of the property. The photos she took showed hundreds of balls of light dancing around the building. I found this quite odd, considering the time of year.

We had been experiencing very heavy rain recently, so the ground was saturated. I can definitely rule out dust being the cause of the photographic anomaly. However, with just a picture at this point, I couldn't say it was anything super-natural, either.

The statue of a fox head greeted us as we approached the door. We entered the building through the main entrance. Immediately, we were all speechless at the marvel of the interior. In the country of Wales, many people believe that if a fox comes anywhere near your home, illness will arrive with it cursing all who enter. I can't say I subscribe to that belief, although Mr. West and his adopted son did die from a very serious illness.

You wouldn't expect it from the outside, but once you step foot inside the building, your mind becomes lost at all of the twists and turns and never-ending rooms. All three of us instantly made a joke about purchasing the place. The house just had some sort of magnetic draw.

The former historic home-turned-restaurant also had a very haunting quality to it. Let's face it, any place that has a large, vintage baby stroller sitting in the middle of the floor for no real reason is creepy.

The first room to our left was to be our base of operations. After unpacking all of the gear, we decided to scout the entire interior and log data ranging from temperature reads to electromagnetic fields. This would give us a base to judge any differences that may occur throughout the night.

Surprisingly, the house was flat as far as electromagnetic fields were concerned. In fact, there weren't any at all. I found that really strange. Typically, there is something. The house had power, yet nothing anywhere gave us the least little bit.

Temperature reads were all over the place however. Gigantic leaps from thirty-five degrees Fahrenheit to fifty-five degrees Fahrenheit only a foot apart. No central air was operating, so the temperature in the house was left to nature outside. So there was another one for the books. Wild and unpredictable temperatures coupled with zero electromagnetic field data.

We made our way into the garden room. This room was obviously used for dances and other events, by the looks of it. Here, we would make our first contact with what we would later learn to be the spirit of the house.

As Allen and I were looking through the doorway into the next room, I was forced to stop in my tracks. I witnessed what appeared to be a dark figure, with the build of a man, vanish around the corner and into the next room. Since we had yet to make it through the entire house, I was a bit concerned that somebody might have broken in, or had been living there illegally. A ghost was the last thing on my mind, but that would change within moments.

Allen and I proceeded through the doorway, only to discover two more open doors. They were both propped open. Allen and I stepped through the doorways and into the other room. However, and to my surprise, when Noelle attempted to enter, the door to the right slammed shut in her face, as if something was trying to keep her from going any farther. This caused Allen and me to jump and turn our attention to the door that was now behind me.

Of course, we tested the door numerous times to see if we influenced it in any way. We stepped on numerous tiles around the door and eventually we were able to re-create the door slamming. Was it us or something else? Time would later answer that question. But for now we needed to continue through the house.

After sweeping through the former kitchen, bar area, and various other rooms, we made our way back to our equipment. It was time to divide up and go our separate ways. We strategically placed each other in areas that would not affect one another. Considering the house was so large, this really wasn't that hard to achieve.

The time was now eight in the evening. Allen took the entire attic section. The attic was lined with a very thick carpet and frankly, was the size of an average home. There were two entrances to the attic. One cascaded beneath the tower, while the other was on the opposite end of the building and was a bit more rustic. Noelle was stationed in the garden room, while I was stationed in the lobby.

Within five minutes, Allen was contacting me on the radio. He said that within just a few feet of him, somebody or something knocked vividly on the wall. I found this interesting, considering he was on the second story. But Allen wasn't alone. Noelle was running tests with her laser grid. The grid is designed to cast hundreds of laser beams through an area, in hopes of exposing a shape or movement. Her laser grid started pulsating and creating strobe-like effects. The device is not designed to do such a thing. But, it would ultimately be what I experienced in the lobby at this time, that would convince me we were not alone.

I was sitting on one of two chairs facing the bar area. Allen contacted me yet again on the radio, asking if I was hearing what he was hearing. Moments before he contacted me I did think I heard a man mumbling and a woman mumbling. Sure enough, Allen suggested the same thing. He said it sounded like it was coming from beneath him at the base of the tower. As I stood up to go investigate, something whistled in my right ear. This caused me to jerk to the right. I was downright shocked.

I proceeded into the other room regardless, to take a look into the voices we were hearing. Unfortunately, I discovered nothing. I returned to the lobby. Instantly I heard heavy footsteps walking across the adjacent room which was considered the living area. Without question, I believed the walking to be from Noelle, since both she and I wear boots, and she would have been returning from the direction.

I stood there waiting for her to come around the corner and enter the lobby, but she never did. I slowly walked over to the doorway of the living room, to see if she or somebody else was in there. I mean the footsteps were so real that anyone in their right mind would have assumed the logical.

I peered inside the room, honestly expecting Noelle to jump out and scare me. But no one was there. I looked up and out the windows of the living room. Through the windows, I could see across the property and into the garden room. Sure enough, I could see Noelle and her flashlight half a building away from me. I instantly turned to look down the other end of the house toward the tower. I could see Allen's flashlight shooting down the staircase. So who just walked through the living room?

At that moment, my stomach sank with excitement and anxiety, and I knew we were not alone. Everybody was accounted for. I immediately contacted them and requested a group gathering to discuss the events that happened within two hours of entering the building.

We met and sat in the living room, to discuss the previous occurrences. While we were doing so, a loud pounding sound came from above, in the attic. It sounded as if something large and heavy hit the floor. But there wasn't anything up there that could have fallen to begin with.

During our discussion, Noelle said she asked the spirit to knock for Allen and to do something flirty with me. Allen did get his knock and I was whistled at. In my mind, we were definitely dealing with something intelligent and something very strong.

After regrouping and collecting ourselves, we went our separate ways again. This time Allen took the living room, Noelle took the attic, and I covered the garden room and kitchen. The time was now eight-thirty in the evening.

About twenty minutes later, I found myself in a commercial kitchen, which was turned into a recreational room.

It was at this point when Allen contacted me on the radio. Allen was asking me if I had been talking to myself recently. Although I was too far away for him to have heard me anyway, I assured him of my silence. He said he heard a man say, "Hey," twice as if someone was trying to gain his attention. I once again assured him of the fact it wasn't me.

Shortly after that, I heard Noelle come across the radio asking Allen if anybody had said "hey" recently. Allen confirmed he had heard the same thing moments earlier; only she had heard it in the attic. It appeared as if our cat-and-mouse playing entity was moving quite quickly through the house.

I left the recreational room and returned to the garden room. Not much was happening for me at this point. But Noelle and Allen were about to witness a whole lot more.

About five minutes had passed. Once again, Noelle came across the radios asking if anybody had made a sound. Both Allen and I confirmed in our respective spots we had not. Noelle captured some sort of animalistic growl up in the attic. She wanted to dismiss it as one of us belching or making some other male sound women have come to love. But that wasn't the case.

She moved up from the lower level of the attic, and into one of the upper levels. Noelle sat on the floor and turned all of her lights off. A hint of light was coming through the large windows. There was just enough light to allow your eyes to focus on the darkness.

Meanwhile, back in the living room, Allen was anxiously waiting for the next confusing twist in this haunting. I believe we all, at this point, were starting to get that familiar feeling of our surroundings turning dark.

Noelle reported a growl, which was definitely something I wasn't prepared to hear happening at this place. That phenomenon was too familiar and too fresh in my mind from previous cases.

As I continued to stand in the garden room, I could see Allen's flashlight waving back and forth through the windows. It was like he was looking for something. Next thing I knew Allen was on the radio again to me. He asked where I was. I confirmed I was in the garden room. Allen was shocked to hear this, as he believed he had just seen me walk through the bar area. I assured him that was impossible. I was not anywhere near the bar. Allen, wishing to dismiss it, asked me to stand still at my location while he went into the bar. He was shocked to see I wasn't there.

Allen eventually found me in the garden room. The look on his face was priceless. He was dumbfounded, to say the least. He honestly believed that I had walked through the bar. If it wasn't me, who was it?

We quickly confirmed with Noelle, on the radios, to make sure she was still in the attic. She was. Noelle was inadvertently documenting something we would later discover on the video the next day. I requested yet another conference with the two investigators in the living room. We started discussing our experiences over the past two hours.

While we were sitting and talking, I saw Allen twitch his right leg. At first I thought he was experiencing a spasm. Noelle and I noticed that, without saying a word, Allen turned his camera on and aimed it down at his feet. We all sat in silence. Allen eventually spoke up and told us he felt something wrap around his calf. He described it as if somebody took their hand and gripped it. Further inspection revealed nothing, but that was definitely worth noting.

The rest of the night produced nothing. It was as if this mysterious man had given us all he had planned for the evening. With the rest of the weekend still ahead of us at Josef's, I couldn't help but consider the potential of residual activity. (A residual haunting occurs when the same activity happens consistently in one location at a predictable time.) In other words, maybe from seven in the evening until nine, which act as the witching hours, so to speak.

Time would tell. Within those two hours, I witnessed a shadow figure, heard whistling and footsteps, and documented other unexplainable sounds. Allen heard voices, saw a figure walking around the bar, heard knocking, and had his leg grabbed. Noelle had a door slammed in her face, and heard voices and growling. We packed up all of the gear and returned to my house, to start transferring footage into the computers.

The next day, we loaded up the car and returned to Josef's. We decided to venture back to the house during the daylight hours to document the building. Noelle immediately started taking photographs around the perimeter again, upon arrival. Allen and I ventured back into the house. We split up and I went to the attic to take notes for my case file.

The house, as a whole, was noticeably colder than it was the night prior. In fact, the building was at least ten degrees colder. This just didn't make any sense to me. The windows were huge and there were plenty of them. Sunlight lit up the entire interior at one in the afternoon. If anything, the house should have been at least ten degrees warmer.

Allen instantly returned to the door that slammed in Noelle's face the night before, to study it a bit more. This was the same area I had witnessed a shadowy figure disappear around the corner moments before it happened.

Meanwhile, Noelle was outside continuing with the documentation. One picture she took in particular raised my brow. At first glance, the anomaly in the photograph appeared to be angelic. With the heavenly light pouring from the open sky over the house, and the glowing halos atop the illuminated figure of an angel—one can only smile at something like this.

Is this a product of simply being in the right place at the right time? Was the lighting just perfect enough to create a mistake on the image? Was this a spirit rising from the ground? Not likely. Regardless, I dismissed it and left it to becoming a conversation piece at best.

Eventually the three of us regrouped. Allen was excited to point out his discovery at the infamous slamming door. He demonstrated to us that no matter what he did, the door would not shut now.

The night before, simply stepping on the right tile caused it to close. That wasn't the case today. He was bouncing up and down, slamming the walls, and doing whatever else he could to make that door move. It refused. We all joined in looking like dancing lunatics in and around the doorway attempting to get it to close. We were unsuccessful.

The three of us divided again to continue documenting during daylight hours. I found myself curious about a closet. Noelle returned to the garden room, and Allen went into the lobby.

As I was exploring the closet under the stairs, Allen screamed from the lobby, "Stephen, get the hell over here!" I said, "What?" He yelled again and with more eagerness, "Get the hell over here, now!" I ran across the room and into the lobby where Allen stood, pointing into the bar, with a pale, white face.

With excitement, he told me he believed somebody to be in there. A male voice had said to him, "Come here," twice from just beyond the door to the bar. As I stood there listening and documenting Allen's experience, both of our heads whipped to the left toward the bar when we heard somebody or something shifting around out of view.

We both sprinted into the bar area only to discover nothing. I immediately started yelling for Noelle and we heard her running from a distance across the garden room floor. She eventually made her way to us and we recounted what had happened. So that blew my previous theory that the activity was locked into a two-hour time frame, from seven in the evening until nine. Here the three of us stood, in broad daylight in the early afternoon, witnessing paranormal phenomena.

We returned to the lobby, intent on not leaving until nightfall. Our intentions were interrupted by the discovery of the baby stroller, sitting in the middle of the floor beneath the tower. Allen quickly pointed it out. Originally, the stroller was against the wall on the opposite side of the closet I was exploring. At some point, in between leaving the closet to meet Allen, to the three of us returning to the lobby, it moved. This stroller moved a great deal, in fact. It was now closer to the lobby door. In other words, it had easily been moved fifteen feet.

We tested the floor for slants. We tested the stroller to see how easy it would move. The wheels were stiff and despite our attempts, we could not make that stroller roll across the floor without physically pushing it the entire way. What was attempting to be said here?

Allen and I returned to the attic to continue research. Noelle swept the kitchen area of the old restaurant. As Allen and I were standing at the top of the steps to the attic, we both noticed what appeared to be a shadow of a person moving at the bottom of the steps. I immediately thought it was Noelle's shadow, so Allen called her on the radio to confirm. Noelle confirmed her location as the kitchen, which was several rooms away.

Allen and I decided to creep down the stairs and see if we could find the source. As we started to approach the kitchen,

a very loud crashing sound, followed by Noelle screaming, occurred. Both Allen and I screamed out to Noelle and
quickly went running to her aid.

When we arrived, she was standing at the foot of the
dumbwaiter. During operations, the dumbwaiter was used as
an elevator to transfer food and other items from one floor
to the next. What startled Noelle was the sound of a handful
of large rocks crashing down through the shaft of the dumbwaiter, smacking the landing below. She had just finished
looking up the shaft when this took place. The rocks had no
origin that made sense, and they literally just missed Noelle.

After the excitement, we went on with our plan to return
to my house. We had hours before nightfall, so reviewing
the previous night's material was on the priority list. Unfortunately, Allen had to return to South Carolina, leaving only
Noelle and myself to continue the rest of the weekend's
research. Noelle and I spent the remainder of the afternoon
reviewing all of the footage captured up until this point.

The following night Noelle and I returned to Josef's for
one final night of research. We started our work in the attic.
We sat on the floor with our cameras also on the floor, actively
filming.

We were sitting in silence, with only the lights from
our cameras lending a view. All of a sudden, the front door
to the building opened and shut, followed by a series of
footsteps. We both glanced at each other, wondering who
entered the building. Was it an unwanted guest?

Since the building was old with wooden floors, sounds carried throughout rather easily. There was no denying that somebody entered the building and started walking through one of the rooms below. We went down the stairs very cautiously to investigate.

I was a little confused, because the front door was still locked and for all intents and purposes, I had the only key. We found no intruder after scouring the first floor, so we returned to the attic.

In the same position on the floor we decided to conduct a communication session. I began asking about who entered the building. We asked if Joe had entered back into his restaurant. It was that question that caused a gasp from the both of us.

As soon as I asked about Joe, the light on my camera just turned plain off. There was no fading out; there was no sign of it coming. It just turned off. Now the importance of that lies in the fact that the only way to turn that light on or off, is with a little switch behind it. Somebody would have to physically flip that switch.

I asked again about Joe, and the light turned back on. This was happening right in front of us. Physical manipulation of a light is not a common thing to witness. After a few more questions, whatever was causing my light to turn off and on decided to leave. Noelle and I decided to split up at this point, with her returning to the first floor and me remaining in the attic.

I moved to the other end of the attic and tried a simple communication with the camera and mounted light. To my delight, it happened again. I was really focusing my questions on Joe West. This would be a huge breakthrough, to prove he was still residing in his old restaurant. He was loved by many and that would certainly make a lot of people happy.

I asked direct questions. "Is this your restaurant?" The light turned off immediately. "Is your name Joe?" The light turned on immediately. I kept going. I asked if whoever I was speaking with could turn the light off, and immediately following that question they did. So then I asked the most important question. "Is your name Joe West?" The light powered immediately on and was brighter than I had ever seen it before. My jaw dropped. I was getting answers through a communication with an electronic light. After all these years, getting something like that, which could potentially validate the identity of a spirit, was worth its weight in gold.

Lastly, I asked for the light to be turned off again and it did just that. I quickly returned to the first floor to show Noelle the footage of what just happened. Shortly after that, we left Josef's and returned to my house.

The investigation was over, but it was a very rewarding one. To finally have the closest thing to answers that we can get was very fulfilling. Out of respect for his close friends and family, I'm not saying that we were in fact experiencing Joe West. All I can do is share with you our experiences, and leave the rest to your interpretation. No matter whether or not Joe is still residing at the Squire's Inn, Josef's, or any of the buildings on the property, Mr. West is very much alive in the hearts that still keep his businesses and memory well known.

ELEVEN

Synchronicity

In many ways I have always been extremely curious about what happens at the moment of death. I have been privileged enough to speak with many individuals who shared in near-death experiences. Even though my journeys have delved more into what happens after death, the beginning is just as important.

Some say they witnessed a bright white light, while others claimed to have seen deceased loved ones. I even heard stories of divine intervention. People witnessing angels, or even God, during near-death experiences has been very common during my research.

Over the past few decades, I have spent a large portion of my life researching the dead and the possibility of intelligent life after death. I will admit, at one point I was highly considering the arrangement of a controlled experiment in which I flatline, just to see what really does happen at that moment.

That sounds crazy to most but true science, curiosity, and exploration know no bounds. If Benjamin Franklin was not willing to be electrocuted, technology might be slightly different now. I mean, what did people think of a man standing in a thunderstorm flying a kite? Of course, maybe I'm just trying to make myself sound less insane.

I would never consider such a dangerous experiment now. So much has changed in my life, including what I have learned and believe about paranormal phenomena, and everything it encompasses.

However, today I am both fortunate and unfortunate enough to share my near-death experience. This experience is more so about prophecy and connections than it is about talking to God or witnessing the infamous light at the end of the tunnel.

I am here to tell you that there was no light at the end of the tunnel. In fact, all to be seen was darkness and all that could be remembered was nothing. Life did not flash before my eyes.

My words are not meant to discredit the experiences of others. I can simply only speak of my experience with conviction, passion, and truth.

The moments before and after my experience are what leave me scratching my head wondering, and once again discovering the amazement of the human body and the possibilities of what could be.

By this point, the paranormal field had completely exhausted me, both mentally and physically. I do have to admit, this event breathed a much needed new life into my slowly fading curiosity.

I suppose at this point, starting at the beginning would be the proper course of action. There is a story here to tell. That story is about my near-death experience that thrust me back into the world of paranormal phenomena and the unexplained. I am writing this chapter exactly one week following the event.

At this point in my life, I had been retired from paranormal research for nearly a year. I can honestly say some aspects of the field I missed, while others were a relief to be rid of.

In late October 2014, I began speaking heavily with paranormal investigator and medical coder, Ryan Lick. Back in 2007, Ryan and I created the P.I.T. Crew, Paranormal Investigation Team. As you can tell by the cases in this book and my previous work, the P.I.T. Crew expanded into a very large and respected team over the years.

Ryan retired from the field in 2012. He contacted me in 2014, stating he had a proposal. That proposal was to accompany him on a new case and investigation, since he was itching to become involved again. I found the offer comical, sentimental, novel, inspiring, and enticing all at the same time.

Going back to the beginnings of my paranormal team was a nostalgic notion. I accepted the offer. I thought, "What the hell." One case wasn't going to hurt anything and completely pull me out of retirement. Besides, reuniting with Ryan would be fun. Over the years, we shared in many great adventures and discoveries, and reliving that for a moment would be a pleasure. Everything was coming full circle.

On Sunday, November 2, 2014, I traveled to Myrtle Beach, South Carolina, to meet up with him. We discussed filming a new case locally, and we ultimately did. Over the next three days, we geared up and walked the walk of paranormal investigating for the first time together in years. That week came and went and almost acted as a prelude of the coming events. I was now returning to the field of paranormal research, and destiny knew it. The following week I was planning to visit Eddie Hughes, another old friend who was involved with the P.I.T. Crew before its dismemberment.

Initially I was to travel to Oak Island, North Carolina, on Tuesday, November 11, 2014, to visit Eddie. My plans unfortunately had to change. I sent him a message explaining that I would not be arriving until the following day. For one reason or another, Eddie never received that message.

The time came and went when I was supposed to have arrived at this house. Eddie called me, concerned that I had not shown up yet. He was worried I had been in a car accident. He said a horrible feeling of dread came over him. I assured Eddie I was fine, and explained that I would be visiting him the following day. Looking back and considering what was to happen, I wish I would have departed that Tuesday for Oak Island. But then again, would it have mattered if we truly have no control of our destiny?

Early the following morning on Wednesday, November 12, I began packing my belongings for the hour and forty-five-minute trip to see Eddie. I loaded the car and prepared to say goodbye to my girlfriend, Noelle.

I gave her a big hug and told her that I loved her. As I started to walk away she said she loved me too. Now that may sound typical or irrelevant, but it is not. Noelle isn't the kind of person that expresses love often. In fact, she rarely says those words, "I love you." Immediately after she said that, I jerked my head around and looked at her. As I said, it was rare to hear her say such a thing so when she did, it was highly noticed.

What she didn't tell me at the time was that she became overwhelmed with the notion that something terrible was about to happen to me. She later told me she believed that moment would be the last time we would ever speak, and that she wanted to say "I love you," just so I knew.

So in a week's time, I had jumped back into the field of paranormal research, heard concern from an old investigator friend that I was going to die, and witnessed my girlfriend believing that Wednesday morning would be the last time she would ever see me. Was that all coincidence, or something far more powerful? Of course, at the moment I thought nothing of it.

I left the area at eight in the morning in a 2008 Chrysler Sebring. The roads were clear, which made the drive rather pleasurable and easy. Mile after mile had passed, and I was finally closing in on Eddie's home. With less than two minutes left of travel time, I made my second-to-last turn onto the highway that would become a personal mystery.

The last thing I remember noticing at this time was the lack of any other vehicles. In fact, there weren't any at all. I owned the road, so to speak. The typically highly trafficked highway connected and led to the bridge that would welcome me to Oak Island. I found it odd that during the morning commute, no other people were driving it. Then it happened. Everything went black.

The car began to accelerate from fifty-five miles per hour to over ninety. After reaching max speed, the car violently shifted completely sideways, causing it to become airborne and land into seven separate rolls and flips, across one hundred and fifty feet of highway.

After rolling seven times, the car slid another fifty yards, until finally stopping completely on its side. The car had turned around to face the opposite direction, while resting vertically on the driver side.

At this moment, the blackness I had succumbed to moments before the accident slowly faded away, revealing a blue and empty ocean. I awoke standing upright in the car, with my arms and head resting out the passenger side window.

Disoriented, I started to realize what had happened. I was in an accident. As I lifted my head, I started to hear the muffled sound of a woman speaking. Everything around me sounded muffled. Her voice slowly became louder, until my eyes focused on her standing on the other side of the car, talking to me.

She was explaining what just happened and was attempting to make sure I didn't move for safety reasons. As she was comforting me I stared at my hands and arms to see hundreds of pieces of glass protruding out of them. Blood was running down the left side of my face, and my hair was blanketed in glass.

Due to the adrenalin in full effect, I felt nothing but numbness. As a determined and hard-headed individual, I explained to the lady that I was fine and could climb out, but she insisted I remain until the paramedics arrived. I asked her if I was the only person involved in the crash and she said I was. She told me I was the only one around at the time. I was honestly relieved about that. She had driven by the accident shortly after it had occurred. These wonderful people stopped to ensure I was alive and called emergency services. Whoever you were, I thank you.

It wasn't long before firefighters, police, and the paramedics arrived. As the firefighters began cutting me out of the vehicle, one of them stated that they believed me to be dead as they approached the devastation. He called the area a "war zone."

A police officer added that he had never in his years on the job witness anybody walk away from an accident such as this one. He said "somebody" was looking out for me, and that I had unfinished business to tend to. The car was completely totaled.

As a part of a responder's job, they must make sure the victim of an accident is in a healthy state of mind. One of the firefighter's asked me how I felt. I chuckled, looked back at the endless trail of debris and said, "I feel like I just walked out of all three *Die Hard* movies." He laughed and yelled back to the other responders to ensure I was conscious and coherent.

I exited the crushed metal coffin and was immediately welcomed by a paramedic strapping a neck brace on me. After loading me up onto the stretcher and into the ambulance, I met EMT Lee Smith. Lee stripped me down and hooked me up to everything Frankenstein was born with. This was a first for me. In my thirty-seven years on this earth, I had never been in an ambulance let alone hooked up to electrode this and electrode that.

Lee had recovered two of my bags from the wreckage, but my fedora was missing. I told him that we weren't leaving until that hat was found. The hat was a very special gift from Noelle years ago, and since many of my closest friends refer to me as "Indy," it was not being left behind. I mean seriously, Indiana Jones never left his hat behind, and neither was I.

Lee jumped out of the ambulance and retrieved my hat. I displayed extreme gratitude as we started our drive to New Hanover Hospital, and I became Lee's personal science experiment. During the ride, he asked me various questions to determine my mental state. This is very common.

He brought up the tattoo on my left arm, which represents the P.I.T. Crew. That of course sparked an entire conversation about the paranormal. Little did Lee know at that time he would be part of this book. It made me think how just months prior, my former head investigator Allen Bess was in a near-death car accident. That too added to the strange feelings.

Following the ghosts and goblins chat, Lee reiterated that I was extremely lucky to be alive. As an EMT, he had seen hundreds of accidents and he said mine would go down in history as entirely amazing. But during all of this conversation, I could not keep two people out of my head. My daughter, Lucidity, and my girlfriend, Noelle, raced through my brain as if I was watching a movie of our lives.

I asked Lee if he had a way for me to contact Noelle. I wanted to contact my daughter as well, but that would have to wait until she was out of school. He supplied me with his personal cell phone, and I called Noelle to break the news. While on the phone with her all I could do was make jokes about the situation. I guess this was my way of coping with a completely traumatizing situation. I remember telling Noelle that I was completely naked and Lee kept touching me. Lee joined in on the fun threatening sexual harassment. I also asked Lee if I was still pretty, since I had yet to see my face, and he assured me I was. Noelle just kept laughing on the phone. She could tell I was going to be all right. Needless to say, the banter between me, Lee, and Noelle made the drive to the hospital much more pleasurable.

Before arriving, Noelle said she was going to start getting ahold of friends and family and in touch with Eddie. He was obviously the closest one to the hospital at that point.

I finally arrived at the destination and a new bed, where more poking and prodding awaited. Labs, x-rays, brain scans, and everything in between revealed absolutely nothing serious. The doctor and accompanying nurses were all astounded at my current physical condition, following such a daredevil stunt. However, it goes without saying that massive bruising, hundreds of slices from the glass, and a hemorrhaging eye were present. A concussion and amnesia were also added to the medical mix. But no broken bones, internal damage, or anything else severe in nature occurred. I am very lucky.

Shortly after all of the tests, I closed my eyes in an attempt to remember anything from the crash. Then I heard a familiar voice. I opened my eyes to see Eddie standing over me. Noelle was able to reach out to him and he rushed to the hospital as soon as possible. As I was picking the glass out of my head and piling it into my lap, Eddie pointed out the fact that the accident took place at 11:11 a.m.

Now for those of you heavily versed in all things paranormal, you are well aware of the 11:11 phenomena. It is believed by numerologists that unusual events taking place at the time of 11:11 occur more often than can be dismissed by coincidence or mere chance. Many subscribers of the phenomena relate this directly to the concept of synchronicity. While this is heavily believed, others tend to relate 11:11 to the presence of a spirit.

There I was, lying in that hospital bed with a pile of glass in my lap, next to an old research colleague, finding myself engrossed in questioning the paranormal. My accident took place during the eleventh month at the eleventh hour and the eleventh minute. At what point does one say, "You can only call it coincidence so many times"? I was originally set to travel on November 11, but had to change my plans to the following day. Did eleven find me anyway? It's strange, I know.

On top of all that, I realized that the drive should have only taken an hour and forty-five minutes at best. So what happened to the other hour and twenty-six minutes? There was a huge gap in time that went completely unexplained. You can't tell me nobody drove down that road for nearly an hour and a half.

The doctor returned to tell me I was being released. I was only in the hospital for a few hours. I got dressed and threw my hat back on and Eddie and I left the building. Eddie drove me the hour and forty-five minutes back home to see Noelle. Everything seemed so surreal. During the entire drive, all I could do was laugh out loud and keep saying that I was alive, over and over.

The following day, Eddie drove to the salvage yard that housed the remains of the car, to take a few pictures for me and gather up anything left inside of the car. He was fortunate enough to hear the official report and pass it on to me.

I was blacked out during the entire event so I knew nothing. I know all of the specifics now, after Eddie was able to obtain them while visiting the wreckage. A thorough investigation was conducted by officials to determine the logistics of the accident. A cause was never determined, and an entire wheel and tire were never found. The hour and twenty-six minutes lost could not be accounted for, either. But was that the end of the mystery crash?

Two days later, I was browsing my friends' profiles on the Internet and came across my paranormal team's old case manager, Valere Bilichka. My mouth dropped when I saw her profile picture was a tattoo of 11:11 on her wrist. Coincidence? At the time, she was unaware of my accident, let alone the bizarre details.

As I viewed her profile more closely, I noticed the night before my accident she was telling God that she was listening and asking what he was trying to tell her. I scrolled further up the page and the day of my accident, Valere wrote a post that said, "I'm feeling unsettled." She would later tell me she was thinking of me at the time. What does all of this mean? There is too much strangeness to ignore.

A few days later, Don Weller called me, out of the blue. I had not spoken with him in years. He said he wanted to call to see how I was doing. Earlier that day he was looking through all of those old pictures from his mother's funeral, wondering if I had more phenomenal stories to share that were like his. Of course, I had to say that I did. Everything was full circle, I suppose. The man and his story I started this book with, would be the man I last spoke with prior to writing the end.

When I look back at starting paranormal research again just a week prior, hearing an old colleague state that he was worried I was in an accident, to Noelle believing that day would be my last, the 11:11 similarities, to the strange feelings and writings from Valere ... how do you not make that a run-on sentence?

I spent the next week in bed, recovering. I had never felt so terrible or helpless in my life. Feeling like you were hit by a tank is not something I would wish on anyone. Staring at yourself in the mirror, with bloody eyes and without facial expression—as if almost lifeless—is a very humble image to witness.

The nights welcomed nightmare after nightmare about the accident. Dreams would show me glimpses of the car rolling from an insider's perspective. I would jolt awake gasping for air, as the car would flip and flip with me inside.

I'm not sure whether these nightmares are a result of the trauma, or if they are in fact giving me a glimpse into the truth behind the accident. They might be visions, they might not. In my head and in my dreams, the same sequence repeats over and over. I am thrown from side to side in the car, and I can see out the passenger side window. The pavement and ocean move as if I'm suspended without motion. I wake up thinking about life instead of death.

What is life anyway? To me life is a series of fortunate and unfortunate memories. I have asked myself every day since why this happened. I have struggled over and over, in attempts to remember any inkling of fact to help explain what happened. I keep begging inside for a memory to appear, that isn't skewed or influenced by too much analysis. We all have a purpose, I suppose. Well, at least it is nice to believe that.

The day of the accident, I realized what the ending of my book should be. My near-death experience is that ending. A ghost hunter who spent his life researching death finally found his own, and that's what it took to discover life.

Whether or not the accident happened for that purpose, the answer hit me at ninety miles per hour. I honestly believed this book to be my last concerning paranormal phenomena. Now, I am not so sure. I guess in the end, nothing ever truly dies.

Afterword

I have to admit this book was a challenge to write. Its predecessor was born effortlessly. All I did was take my most productive and interesting case files and place them across a couple hundred pages, respectfully and authentically. In fact, I never even intended it to be a book.

But this one was much different. I wanted to show a more human side to all of this, and something less mechanical. I wanted to place you more inside my head, and less behind a battery-operated device. Although the study and bells and whistles are present, they are a little less overwhelming, this time around.

The majority of what you read materialized straight from journal entries and audio recordings, taken at the time of the investigations or experiences. That is a point I can't stress enough. Certainly now, I can look back and question specific elements of each, but at the same time, some things are best left alone.

The field of real paranormal research is so diluted by the mainstream media. Film and television have taken an interest and exploited it to the point of ridiculousness. I know, because I have been in that world, where my words and actions are scripted for me.

That in itself was one of the reasons I found this book so difficult to complete. Much of what I shared is beyond believability and above the stereotypical norm of traditional paranormal house calls.

These stories are true and I deserved to share them. I was going to put this out there and let people see what it is like to run after anything laced in the supernatural, without any restrictions. I also lowered the personal barrier a bit, and shared more of what this life can do to a person or in this case, what it did to me.

The other reason was simply the time it took to gather up interesting and productive cases to share with you. For every one case in this book that yielded results, dozens of others were left as a blank canvas.

I started this edition years ago, immediately following the previous release. Just like the book before it, the investigations within took years to document. This was not written in a month.

In many ways, the path I choose to lead is a huge crutch when it comes to writing. I write about paranormal research, and the results taken from the field do not meet conclusions overnight. It takes hundreds and hundreds of cases to find those rare gems that become the stories I share.

I am fortunate to have some of the best minds to work with. I am also extremely fortunate to be respected and called upon for cases and access to locations most would dream of. I have worked cases for the military, for politicians, for the average Joe, and for myself. That is the reality. I didn't have a producer lining up scripted locations to play pretend in. I, as well as many others, lived this reality, and it takes a toll on you without the paycheck. But that's enough tooting of one's horn.

What I am trying to say is that I am very grateful to have the opportunities and respect that I do. Even though I have seen a lot, I can't say I have even come close to seeing it all. One day it is this, and the next day it is that, and ultimately that's the beauty of this field—and a blessing in disguise.

I have traveled all around, investigating suburban homes to conducting military reconnaissance in treacherous territory. I have gone after the ghosts and attempted to track down the monsters. All I can say at this point concerning the research, is there remains a crowded mind of questions without answers.

In mid-November 2013, almost immediately following the Josef's case, I officially retired from the field of paranormal research. Seventeen years of living in the darkness had taken its toll on me, and it was time to move on. My heart was black to the idea of continuing on.

I was becoming unhealthy and desensitized to the real world I was so eager to close my eyes to. Unfortunately, I have more scars than you could ever imagine, and not a one of them came from a ghost. When you truly, and maybe foolishly, devote your life to the dead, you sacrifice a piece of life you can never get back.

Do I regret anything? Yes, maybe a few things I am not ready to talk about. But for the most part, I made these decisions and was willing to walk through whatever door opened, as a result of it.

Do I feel like a fool? Yes, I do. I spent so much time chasing after things I couldn't see, I became blind to the things I could.

On the human side of things, I've been through a lot over the years. There is another side of me that actually has a "normal" life. That car crash was a huge awakening for me. This book might not have seen its end.

But I look back at all of those memories—good and bad. They didn't flash before my eyes during the wreck. They flash before my eyes every day, because there are people in my life that are absolutely the best and wonderful experiences I've been fortunate enough to have, who cannot be forgotten.

I never expected that my work would go beyond my own filing cabinet, years ago. I never expected to see my face on television shows, news broadcasts, and in publications. I would have never thought that I would be interviewed on hundreds of radio shows.

But it happened. You believed in me and my purpose. For that I am truly a humbled soul. I can't say my retirement will last forever and I can't say it won't. Life has been full of surprises, and many of the experiences I have had throughout my life came without expectation. This has been an adventure of learning, excitement, heartache, failure, and triumph. I am, without a doubt, a different person than I was ten years ago, for better or worse.

I have met a lot of like-minded people over the years, and I cherish their friendships dearly. I plan to continue writing. I still have much to say and share. But with my first book, I wanted to show you the technical side of what I do. With this book, I wanted you to see a more human side. The next could go any direction and time will certainly tell. We all grow.

With all of that being said, you have to dance with what brought you. I would like to give special thanks to those who have picked me up when I have fallen down. I would like to thank those who, no matter the circumstances, no matter my condition, both physically and mentally, have always been and always will be there for me. You all have tracked through the thickest mud with me. You have cried alongside and bled with me. Many of you have seen my hell and never hesitated to join me there. You trusted me and openly supported everything I was doing. Your support and enthusiasm warmed my heart in a way that will never be forgotten.

To all others, thank you for reading my books and hopefully finding a little piece in each that makes you think, or even offers you a new perspective.